Political Discourse in Exile

Political Discourse in Exile

KARL MARX
and the Jewish Question

Dennis K. Fischman

AMHERST   The University of Massachusetts Press

Copyright © 1991 by
The University of Massachusetts Press

All rights reserved

Printed in the United States of America

LC 90-24603

ISBN 0–87023–746–2

Designed by David Ford

Set in ITC Bookman Light

Printed and bound by Thomson-Shore

Library of Congress Cataloging-in-Publication Data
Fischman, Dennis K., 1958–
    Political discourse in exile : Karl Marx and the Jewish
question / Dennis K. Fischman.
      p. cm.
    Includes bibliographical references and index.
    ISBN 0–87023–746–2 (alk. paper).
    1. Communism and Judaism.   2. Marx, Karl, 1818–
1883.   3. Judaism—Influence.   I. Title.
HX550.J4F57   1991
335.4—dc20   90–24603
                                        CIP

British Library Cataloguing in Publication data are
available.

An earlier version of chapter 1 appeared as "The Jewish
Question about Marx," in *Polity* 21, no. 4 (Summer 1989).

Contents

Acknowledgments

It was almost purely a matter of chance that I began my gradu-
ate work at the University of Massachusetts at Amherst in Sep-
tember 1981. Yet if I had studied political theory anywhere else,
with a different set of teachers, this book would never have been
written. Jerry King, a superb educator, encouraged me to find out
what mattered to me and to take it seriously: for a teacher, no
higher praise is possible. Jean Bethke Elshtain helped me make
sense to myself and forced me to make sense to others. Robert
Paul Wolff lent me his skepticism and his enthusiasm. William E.
Connolly, from my first day as his student onward, challenged
me, confused me, and changed the way I think. Joan Cocks of
Mount Holyoke College read the early chapters of the manuscript
and commented in detail, and I am grateful. I also wish to thank
Gerard Braunthal for his support.

While teachers are indispensable, for true study the Jewish
tradition offers this advice: "Get yourself a friend." Shane Phelan
and I have been friends throughout some of the most tumultuous
years of our lives. We have argued passionately, laughed uproari-
ously, and sat stock still, looking at each other, enchanted by a
glistening idea neither of us would have seen alone. I finished this
book so Shane could read it.

I would also like to thank Doc Bachman, Rom Coles, Kim Cur-
tis, Bob Siegfried, Philip White, Rabbi Arnold Jacob Wolf, the
Caucus for a New Political Science, Havurat ha-Ruach (North-
ampton, Mass.), and many members of New Jewish Agenda. The
staff at Rosemont College gave clerical assistance, and Alice Kes-
wani helped prepare the final version of the manuscript, for
which she has my special thanks.

The University of Massachusetts Press guided me through the

viii   Acknowledgments

publication process with patience and good will. Bruce Wilcox, Richard Martin, Clark Dougan, Pam Wilkinson, Brenda Hanning, and Catlin Murphy all deserve my gratitude. I thank Peter Rutkoff and an anonymous reader for their constructive criticism. Chapter 1 was previously published in the Summer 1989 issue of *Polity*: I acknowledge its staff and readers.

My parents, Melvin and Faye Fischman, show their influence in everything I do: they are my first and best teachers. Breaking with convention, I will try to hold them and all my teachers responsible for the shortcomings of this book—until they begin to teach me better.

For two years, Rona Fischman lived in a city she could not stand while I finished the dissertation that became this book—I guess she must like me or something. *Political Discourse in Exile* is dedicated to her.

Political Discourse in Exile

Introduction

SUPPOSE, PLAYFULLY, as a kind of parlor game, one tried to answer the question, What single phrase of Karl Marx's tells us most about his life and thought? The reply for which I would hold out comes not from *Capital*, or *The Communist Manifesto*, or any of his work that the public and scholars know best. I would point to a letter Marx wrote to his son-in-law Paul Lafargue in 1882, one year before he died. In that note, he gibes, "What is certain is that I am no Marxist."[1]

What did Marx mean by this extraordinary statement? Even before making itself understood, it displays the man's abiding love of paradox—his irresistible pull toward ironic formulations and his fascination with contradictory realities. Once in context, the remark speaks of another, perhaps less endearing trait: his biting sarcasm. For the "Marxists" he puts at a distance are his would-be disciples, the leaders of the workers' movement in France, whom he disowns because of their reformist and anarchist leanings. The old lion devours the young whelps. To a theorist who is also a revolutionary, his followers must be his most prized possessions, since only through their efforts can his goals be expressed in practice. Yet incredibly, one can hear "the cutting disdain with which he pronounced the word *bourgeois*"[2] ringing through Marx's sneer at "Marxists."

Granted, Marx never took political disagreements lightly. Although a doting father and loving (if unfaithful) husband, over his ideological opponents he often sat as a grim and implacable judge, pursuing them relentlessly in polemic after polemic. Still, I would argue, Marx's declaration "I am no Marxist" is there to teach us something crucial about his theory and our relation to it.

3

Without relinquishing its immediate message, we could go on to read this remark very differently. If we chose, we could hear Marx repudiating with this statement, not only those particular interpreters, but also all the copyists and critics who would try in later years to make "Marxism" into a system. His continual revisions are as much a part of Marx's writings as the texts themselves. "I find unsatisfactory a work written four weeks before and rewrite it completely," he observes. This is no mere quirk, no annoying personal tic: it is a philosophy of writing. "It is self-evident," he writes, "that an author, if he pursues his research, cannot publish *literally* what he has written six months previously."[3] The passage of time, Marx presumes, brings change and growth to the writer if he or she is fortunate; to the text, it always does. The meaning of what is written lies in the future.

If we pursue this line of thought, we can read none of Marx's many books and essays as a finished work. Each refers to the next, to all others, and to works he never lived to write or (perhaps) even to imagine. Just as he labored over Hegel, Feuerbach, and Ricardo, looking for questions demanding to be asked and riddles crying out to be solved, so, too, did Marx exploit his own work as a mother lode of gaps and contradictions awaiting further inquiry. Writing his work, Marx also read it; writing new texts, he read through and beyond old ones. Thus, Marx is no "Marxist." But those of his readers who codify his thinking, whether as votaries or heretics, are. And they have not learned all that Marx has to teach.

An amusing piece of wordplay, but . . . is this any way to draw conclusions about Marx's theory? Even for the sentence in question, we have one perfectly sound explanation already: a political disagreement between Marx and the French socialists. Did he mean anything else by it? We have no obvious reason to think so. After all, it takes an enormous leap of the imagination to read one flippant comment as a theory in brief; besides, it requires setting the immediate circumstances or context of the remark to one side. Above all, even if Marx considers his work an open-ended, self-referential, meaningful totality, is he right to do so? Does any theorist have the right to set down the standard by which his or her own work will be judged? Unless we treat Marx's theory as a set of positions taken, as we do with every other political theory, how can we come to terms with it at all?

These are serious questions indeed—perhaps, too serious. By any chance, might we entertain the possibility of ignoring them? I think there are good reasons for us willingly to suspend our disbelief in the reading we have pursued so far. For one, it is simply not true that we discovered Marx's philosophy of writing in the phrase "I am not a Marxist" alone. That would have been impossible. In order even to think of connecting them, we first had to become aware of Marx's work habits and publishing history as well as his way of approaching his own and other people's previous writings, and regard them as a problem. At the same time, we had to wonder what in the world "I am not a Marxist" means, coming from Marx. Only that initial noticing and wondering could move us to join the perplexing phrase to the odd theoretical attitude in order to search for their shared interpretation.

We did not explain "I am not a Marxist" by a previously known theory, nor did we prove the existence of the theory by the single citation. Instead, we groped about for a way into Marx's thinking that would let us make sense of both, together. Finding that way in, our next step should be to travel it back through the dense undergrowth of Marx's theory in general, to see whether it can lead us to an understanding of that theory that is at least as clear and convincing as any other approach. There is nothing strange in this procedure: it is a variant of the famous hermeneutic circle, with the difference that we start by puzzling over what we do not understand about the text rather than clarifying what we do.[4]

Suppose, then, we go ahead and try to apply our tentative insight to the task of understanding Marx. Inevitably, at the same time that we inquire, Is this really how Marx conceived of what he was doing? we will be asking and framing a definite opinion on the related question, Was he right? For if Marx can plausibly be thought to have intended to include future developments of his theory in the theory itself, then his intention is part of the theory. To disregard that intention (as distinct from disbelieving it) would be to commit a breach of faith. If we come to affirm that Marx did regard his work as stretching into the future, beyond the printed page, then we would have to treat that self-definition as a kind of "performative utterance": that is, it does what it says it does. When an authorized official says, "I now pronounce you man and wife," it makes no sense to ask if he or she is telling the truth.[5] Similarly, if Marx intends that we readers should get caught on the surface irregularities of his theory, not plane them down to a smooth superficiality, how can we legitimately do otherwise? To read Marx literally is to falsify him. In order to read him truly, we must lend him the use of our imaginations.

As Louis Dupré writes in his work on Marx's critique of culture:

> The lasting effectiveness of Marx's analysis invites us to an active dialogue. This distinguishes him from past figures whose impact has long been absorbed by our culture. Descartes steered modern thought in a new direction, but he has ceased to inspire cultural innovation. Marx's critique continues to challenge our attitudes today. He remains a living partner in the sociocultural discussion. But precisely on that ground he demands to be treated as a contemporary—that is, critically rather than deferentially.[6]

Certainly, this philosophy of writing we have ascribed to Marx grants him an incomparable advantage over the straitened formulations of other thinkers. By accepting it, we agree to "learn from" Karl Marx not only what he teaches us explicitly,[7] but also anything we infer or invent to make sense of his teachings. In return, Marx becomes extraordinarily vulnerable. On the same assumptions, he has no choice but to bend to any plausible construction with which we burden his theory.

There are limits, of course, both to our license and to our debt, his obligation and his claim to respect. An argument can oppose Marx's logic instead of restoring it, or clash with his themes, not harmonize with them. The burden of proof shifts—it falls on those who would narrow the orbit of Marx's teachings—but it is not done away with altogether. Still, the boundaries of Marx's theory, like its persuasiveness, finally remain a matter of judgment, not proof. They are "essentially contestable," and so each reader's decision on where they lie is intimately related to his or her own identity and concerns in a way that argument alone is unlikely to change.[8]

In this essay, then, I will take Marx at his word and explore his social and political theory from a non-"Marxist" perspective. Practically speaking, that means I will start out from one of the many unsolved riddles about Marx's thought and try to read through and beyond it, as he might have, in order to learn where the theory has to go next.

Now, there is no more obscure question about Marx's theory than its relation to his Jewish background. Jews and Judaism provide a potent symbol for the organization of Marx's political thinking. It is to the "Jewish question" that Marx turns when he announces his break with Left Hegelianism, and again when he renews his fire at Bruno Bauer in *The Holy Family*. In the succinctly worded *Theses on Feuerbach*, Marx takes the time to chide his opponent for considering practical activity "only in its dirty-judaical manifestation."[9] Overt references to Judaism are fewer in his later writings, yet on careful reading, even *Capital* exhibits the stance Marx had earlier identified as "Jewish": the assertion of present human need against the claims of philosophical idealism that it had already made humanity free.

Yet studies of Marx tend to deny *any* relation between Marx's Jewishness and his theory. The most simplistic account is offered by Saul Padover: Marx was an antisemite, therefore he could have learned nothing from Judaism. "Marx's hatred of Jews was a canker which neither time nor experience ever eradicated from his soul." It "reflected nearly total ignorance, possibly willful, of the lives and faith of the people from whom he descended."[10]

I will demonstrate in chapter 1 that Marx is nothing like a simple antisemite, that his attitude is much more ambivalent than it would first appear, and that on the whole, he comes out supporting the claims of Judaism against those of Christianity. All this, however, is somewhat beside the point. Antisemitism in no way precludes learning from the Jewish tradition, especially internalized antisemitism on the part of one who was born into that tradition. The really interesting question would be: How did Marx's conflicted relationship to his own Jewishness affect the manner of his learning from Jewish thought?

This is where more serious objections arise. According to one objection, marginality, not Jewishness, was the element of Marx's background which shaped his theory. "Marx was all the more predisposed to take a critical look at society as he came from a milieu that was necessarily excluded from full social participation," writes David McLellan. Stressing the outsider status of nineteenth-century German Jews downplays the *content* of Jewish identity as an influence on Marx, which is just what McLellan means to do. He contends that Marx shows "virtually no sign of Jewish self-consciousness in his published writings or in his private letters," and adds:

> Some students of Marx believe they have found the key to Marx's whole system of ideas in his rabbinic ancestry; but although some of his ideas—and even life-style—have echoes of the prophetic tradition, this tradition is more or less part of the Western intellectual heritage; and it would be too simplistic to reduce Marx's ideas to a secularized Judaism. [11]

Shlomo Avineri roots Marx's theory firmly in one specific part of that "Western intellectual heritage," namely "his Hegelian antecedents." Hegel's philosophy, he argues, is "a unique synthesis between the theological traditions of the Judeo-Christian [*sic*] world and the intellectual achievements of the Enlightenment." Any apparent likeness between Marx and Jewish thought is a by-blow of Marx's attachment to Hegel. In order to grant any importance whatever to Marx's Jewishness, Avineri first demands a solution to "the problem of Marx's own awareness of those specific traditions held responsible for his own views." [12]

These accounts of Marx's intellectual roots proclaim a widely held orthodoxy: the irrelevance of Judaism to Marx's theory. [13] If Marx's marginal social position can explain his political commitments and his grasp of Hegel produces the outlines of his thought, then why bother investigating Judaism? Far easier to endorse the following summary by a sociologist of religion:

> Marx was not a Jew in any religious, national, or cultural sense. He knew nothing about Judaism and showed no interest in the subject. Nor did he "inherit" any rabbinic or talmudic qualities or properties. These are acquired skills, no more transmitted by birth than a knowledge of philosophy or geology would be. [14]

What are we to make of these objections? As literary theorist Susan Handelman writes, "To try to prove that a Jewish background has some influence on even the most avowedly secular Jews is a difficult and complicated task." [15] I shall not attempt it here, even though I believe (and will show in chapter 1) that the "irrelevance" argument is much overstated.

Instead of tracing influence, I will outline the structural affinities between Marx's thought and the worldview of the Jewish tradition. Marx's ontology, I suggest in chapters 2 and 3, makes more sense read through the particular notions of being and becoming, space and time, thought and action which animate the Hebrew Bible. Likewise, what Bertell Ollman calls Marx's "philosophy of internal relations" and the peculiar use of language it entails seem almost familiar in a Hebraic context.[16] Marx's insistence that philosophers cannot know the world by contemplating it but only by relating to other human beings echoes the biblical theme of dialogue. His reading of history as a dialectic of needs follows the pattern set in the Torah for a continuing effort to hallow the world.

In chapter 4, I view Marx's philosophy of writing in light of *midrash*, the classic Jewish style of hermeneutics. As with Marx's ontology, the purpose of the comparison goes beyond mere similarity toward the discovery of new meaning. It makes a difference if we find that Marx's theory becomes richer in the matrix of the Jewish tradition than in the Greco-Christian tradition of philosophy taken alone. The difference that it makes starts to appear in our changed conception of Marx's overall project. Chapter 5 attempts to reconstruct that project, drawing on the added understanding that an acquaintance with the plotline of the biblical narrative, with its themes of exile and return, bestows. Finally, in the conclusion, I consider how we, today, must reinterpret Marx's task in order to fulfill it.

When I suggest that certain elements of Jewish thought can serve us as an appropriate context in which to read Marx, I do not wish to deny the usefulness of other interpretive approaches. The way we shall take here, however, is virtually unexplored. In its pursuit, we may find ourselves far afield, even temporarily out of sight of the well-trodden paths of Marx scholarship. That need not bother us. We know the way back, and we can leave it for later to try to trace where we have been on the same map. For now, we must simply follow our own trail.

Nor need we stumble over the mistaken notion that if an idea of Marx's is not solely or exclusively Jewish, we cannot read it in the context of the Jewish tradition. Part of what it means to partake of a tradition is to be sensitive to how one part of that tradition comments on, and is enriched by, all the others. Ideas are not free agents. We understand their content and their import in relation to the web of other thoughts and themes in which we are accustomed to find them. If we decide to relate Marx's writings to Jewish thought, we open ourselves to a whole world of allusions and associations, and we begin to make out an already ongoing conversation in which old statements may resonate with new meanings. The question is not whether Marx wants to be a part of this conversation, but whether we do.

One more caveat is in order. When I propose to explore the structural affinities between Marx's thinking and Jewish thought, I am not subscribing to any of the rival structuralisms or poststructuralisms which have recently beset social theory. As I understand Marx, dichotomies like "structure versus event" or even "structure versus subjectivity" offer little help in engaging with him. Furthermore, just as Marx is not a Marxist, none of the leading figures of poststructuralism accepts the label or the limits of their followers. When I refer to Derrida, Bloom, Foucault, or Althusser, I draw on their teachings alone and not the halo of scholastic disputes surrounding them.

As for the tack I am taking here, a non-"Marxist" approach to Marx through the question of his relation to Judaism, it leads immediately toward two potential dangers: misreading Judaism to make it foreshadow Marx, or misreading Marx to make him somehow more Jewish. With respect to the first, presenting a living religious culture as an ideology: to some extent, limitations of scope make this unavoidable. To compensate, I will differentiate wherever relevant among movements and periods in Jewish history. I will try at all times to indicate when I am offering a controversial perspective on Jewish belief, whether that perspective is my own, Marx's, or belongs to someone else. Yet controversy is an integral part of the Jewish tradition, and innovations can sometimes claim the authority of something "already told to Moses at Sinai"—even mine.[17]

As for the opposite danger, what McLellan calls "reduc[ing] Marx's ideas to a secularized Judaism": I confess, I do not see exactly how it could be done. Certainly, it is no part of my intention. Indeed, it runs directly counter to a crucial feature of my own interpretation.

For I understand Marx as a political thinker in exile: a man trying to express the truths of one reality in the language and grammar of another. Marx develops his theory in the process of criticizing Western philosophy and political economy. To a great extent, he makes the discourse of these fields his own; their agenda becomes his. Yet Marx writes as if his Jewish conceptions of the centrality of human need, the potentially meaningful nature of the world, and the pivotal role of human action were obvious to his opponents and his readers alike. Even more: he writes as if his ideas were the only ideas, as if any other point of view could be dismissed as the product of bad faith or delusion. By misunderstanding the rootedness of his thought, Marx misleads himself about the kind of audience his words would find—and therefore, about the prospects of imminent revolution.

Mistaking his own predicament, caught between what can be done and what must be, compelled to write, fated not to be heard, Marx never found himself a home in either philosophy or Jewish thought. His work remains unfinished, a legacy to generations of seekers. If we attempt to recover the meanings of Marx's thought which emerge from the context of the Jewish tradition, it is not to simplify his project but to elaborate it, for the purpose of taking it up anew.

In our own search for meaning, and for freedom, we still have much to learn from Marx. The theme of exile, which sounds in his work, resonates in our own endeavors; so, too, does the reality of exile which describes his memorable life. To quote the most subtle of his biographers:

> Karl Marx was not merely a revolutionary, a theorist of socialism, or a figure in the history of economic or political theory. He was—and remains—an exemplary presence in the development of modern consciousness, whose significance is not exhausted by the truth or falsity of the specific doctrines he propounded. His life exemplifies the link that joins thought to action, and the gap that separates them. [18]

Because in modernity we live our lives in the midst of that divide, struggling to forge that link—because we, too, are strangers in a land not our own—our dialogue with Marx goes on.

Four Jewish Questions about Marx

MOST OF US who study Marx today read him se-
riously for the first time in college, where professors routinely
assign the essay, "On the Jewish Question." Having placed it in
front of us, however, they immediately snatch it away. We are
instructed to read the essay in a special way, one that we would
not have thought of alone: as an attack on the liberal notion
of freedom. The secondary texts agree with this interpretation.
"The central problem" of "On the Jewish Question," according to
David McLellan, has little to do with the Jews; rather, it is "the
contemporary separation of the state from civil society and the
consequent failure of liberal politics to solve social questions."[1]
Louis Dupré defines the essay's theme this way:

> Attacking Bauer's proposal of total secularization as the solution of
> the Jewish problem in Germany, Marx claimed that the secular,
> democratic state is *the* modern version of the religious illusion. It
> maintains the same relation of *apparent* dominance and *real* sub-
> servience to civil society which exists between the religious sphere
> and the profane world.[2]

What we are encouraged to learn from "On the Jewish Question," therefore, is what Marx objected to in the liberal idea of
freedom and what he would offer in its place. Jews and Judaism
enter the picture only incidentally. We read in McLellan that the
"Jewish question" itself makes "a convenient peg on which to
hang his [Marx's] criticism of the liberal state." Dupré gives it a
minor place within Marx's general critique of religion. Together

12

with Shlomo Avineri, who ignores Judaism altogether in his major work on Marx, these writers reflect what has become the orthodox approach to "On the Jewish Question." It is this orthodoxy that is taught in schools—in place of the article itself.

Certainly, there are good reasons why this reading has appealed to teachers. It has proved enormously powerful in extracting theoretical resources from the rough terrain of Marx's rhetoric. It also relieves the instructor of having to discuss a delicate subject about which he or she may know little. Yet if our object is to understand what freedom means to Marx, and how his idea of emancipation differs from liberal ideas, then the standard reading of "On the Jewish Question" leaves out an entire dimension of the problem, precisely because it skips over Marx's own relation to Judaism.

If we were to read "On the Jewish Question" for the first time, naively, we surely would not blurt out, What is Marx saying about freedom? How does he relate the state to civil society? Instead, we could almost not help asking, Why is this man so antisemitic?

That he *is* antisemitic, the essay appears to leave no doubt. True, in its first, longer installment (responding to Bruno Bauer's book *Die Judenfrage*), Marx's animus reveals itself less blatantly. He sins by omission only, repeating without comment Bauer's claim: "The Jew, by his very nature, cannot be emancipated . . . since he opposes his illusory nationality to actual nationality, his illusory law to actual law."[3]

In the second section, however, Marx seems fairly to bristle with anti-Jewish sentiments. He begins by substituting for Bauer's inquiry into "the capacity of present-day Jews and Christians to become free" the question: "What specific social element is it necessary to overcome in order to abolish Judaism?"[4] For Marx, that is the real problem beside which the petty manner of civil rights for Jews fades into insignificance. Indeed, "in the final analysis, the *emancipation* of the Jews is the emancipation of mankind from *Judaism*."[5] Jews, Marx seems to be saying, can only become free when, as Jews, they no longer exist.

We would be mistaken to think Marx advocates either religious assimilation or genocide as a solution. Marx does not take the

Jewish faith that seriously. If religion in general (read: Christianity) is the opium of the people, in Marx's view, the Jewish religion in particular lacks the power to produce even illusory happiness. Religious Judaism is a mere nullity which "would evaporate like some insipid vapour in the real life-giving air of society," if society were as it should be. Indeed, totally disregarding the content of Jewish belief, Marx identifies Judaism completely with the economic arrangements he finds prevailing in capitalist society, and the abolition of Judaism with the transcendence of capitalism.

> Let us consider the real Jew: not the *sabbath Jew*, whom Bauer considers, but the *everyday* Jew.
> Let us not seek the secret of the Jew in his religion, but let us seek the secret of the religion in the real Jew.
> What is the profane basis of Judaism? *Practical* need, *self interest*. What is the worldly cult of the Jew? *Huckstering*. What is his worldly god? *Money*.
> Very well: then in emancipating itself from *huckstering* and *money*, and thus from practical Judaism, our age would emancipate itself.[6]

"Money," writes Marx, "is the jealous god of Israel, beside which no other god may exist." In order to speak of the growing power of money over politics, Marx carries the association to its outer limits: society, he declares, has become "Jewish."

> The god of the Jews has become secularized and has become the god of this world. The bill of exchange is the real god of the Jew. His god is only an illusory bill of exchange.

On this account, Marx finds nothing incongruous in speaking of "the effective domination of the Christian world by Judaism." On this point, he can even quote Bauer with approval: "In theory, the Jew is deprived of political rights, while in practice he wields tremendous power and exercises on a wholesale scale the political influence which is denied him in minor matters."[7]

"The Jew" functions as a symbol in Marx's thinking. He does not really mean to subscribe to a Jewish conspiracy theory. The overtones of this essay are still ominous, however, and as readers we are entitled to ask why, if Marx meant only to criticize liberalism for neglecting the power of money, he saw fit to drag the Jews into the argument.

I

The question as to the reason for Marx's antisemitism brings a second, equally troubling question in its wake. Why is it that writers on Marx leave his anti-Jewish slurs unchallenged, even unexamined? Not *unnoticed*, certainly: nearly every commentator mentions antisemitism in passing (again with Avineri as a notable exception). They bring it up, however, only to denounce it or excuse it—never to confront it as a problem in itself. It is as if there never were a "Jewish question," as if the substance of what Marx says about Jews was entirely unimportant.

We take McLellan's book once again as the epitome of how Marx's anti-Jewish harangue is usually treated. "It is true," he admits, "that a quick and unreflective reading of, particularly the briefer second section, leaves a nasty impression." Furthermore, Marx is known to have "indulged elsewhere in anti-Jewish remarks—though none as sustained as here." On the other hand, McLellan argues, in the same year Marx wrote "On the Jewish Question," he lent his support to a petition *for* Jewish rights, commenting to his associate Arnold Ruge, "The point is to punch as many holes as possible in the Christian state and smuggle in rational views as far as we can." In fact, suggests McLellan, the whole antisemitic line of thought in Marx's essay may be largely accidental. "The German word for Jewry—*Judentum*—has the secondary sense of commerce and, to some extent, Marx played on this double meaning."[8] To some extent!

The implicit conclusion is clear. Marx's antisemitism has been exaggerated, and in any case is tangential to his main point. No harm done in ignoring it. Time to move on.

The problem with this way of reading Marx is that it takes for granted the same dubious assumption that Marx relies on: that we can learn something from "the Jewish question" without actually paying attention to it. At first glance, it might seem Marx is simply following the same procedure we used earlier in interpreting his utterance, "I am not a Marxist." Out of the social fact that the German Jews seek emancipation, he divines a new meaning: that the liberal state must ever fail to create freedom for all of its citizens because it depends for its own power on an inherently unfree and unequal economic system. In our exegesis, however, we kept the original situation in plain view even while we departed from it. Our resulting interpretation added a new layer of meaning to the tension between Marx and his followers; at the same time, it opened up the new question of how Marx wrote. Marx's reformulation of Bauer's topic makes the original controversy invisible—and the Jews, its subject, along with it. What is more, by adhering to Marx's explicit argument, commentators like McLellan obscure the Jewish question of "On the Jewish Question" even further. All this is too bad, for two reasons.

The first is that when a Jew makes antisemitic remarks and no one disputes them, even the well-meaning will wonder if they are not true after all. For "there is probably no individual, from Abraham and Moses to Herzl and Martin Buber, to whom the epithet 'Jew' has been more persistently applied than Marx."[9]

Born in 1818 in the ancient city of Trier, Karl Marx descended from three centuries of rabbis on both sides of his family tree, including scions of the illustrious Heschel and Katzenelenbogen families.[10] His father, Heschel ha-Levi Marx, changed his name to Heinrich upon his conversion to Christianity, about a year before Karl was born. Heschel's baptism was a matter of economics, not faith: the Prussian government had begun to enforce its requirement that all lawyers be Christians. *Paris vaut bien une messe.* The Jewish faith, too, had held little attraction for him. A staunch rationalist, in philosophy a follower of Kant, Heschel believed in a simple deism, "the faith of Newton, Locke, and Leibniz."[11] Yet his ties to the Jewish people remained firm enough that in 1815, he drafted a long memorandum to protest an edict aimed at bankrupting Jewish moneylenders, while in the following year he unsuccessfully sought a special exemption to allow him to keep both his religion and his livelihood.[12] In all probability, Karl Marx's father was one of the many Jews who converted "without really relinquishing their family and social ties with the [Jewish] community."[13]

Karl's mother, Henriette Pressburg Marx, remained even more stubbornly entrenched in her Jewish identity. The daughter of a Dutch rabbi, she probably spoke Yiddish in her parents' home; whether she continued doing so in Trier is uncertain, but we know from her letters that she never bothered to learn to write German grammatically.[14] She resisted conversion until 1825, nearly eight years after her children's baptisms (including that of Karl, who was then six and a half). From her correspondence, it is clear that the Marxes retained their Jewish contacts, especially with Heschel's sister-in-law, the widow of the rabbi of Trier, and her children. Even in 1853, a full eighteen years after adopting the Lutheran church, Henriette could write to her own sister about Karl's sister's departure for South Africa: "And it seems that the lot of the People is again being realized in me—that my children should be scattered throughout the world."[15]

As for Marx himself, one biographer asserts:

> Karl Marx spent his earliest years in a family whose religious division was a witness to the way society's power over men's livelihoods could play tricks on their self-conceptions, forcing them to deny their convictions.[16]

Whether for that reason or some other, Marx never studied Hebrew, even though the language was taught at the *Gymnasium* he attended by a (Christian) member of the Casino Club, a pro-French organization to which Heschel Marx also belonged.[17] In Berlin, however, Karl did learn jurisprudence under Eduard Gans, one of the founders of the *Wissenschaft des Judentums* movement, and it was under that instructor that he first paid serious attention to Hegel.[18] In later years, Marx would cross paths with an extraordinary selection of "non-Jewish Jews," including Heinrich Heine, Moses Hess, Ferdinand Lassalle, and Ludwig Kugelmann.[19] He also made a friend of the rationalist Jewish historian Heinrich Graetz.

More crucial for our purposes than Marx's relations with other Jews, however, is the fact that others recognized Marx as a Jew. A sponsor of the *Rheinische Zeitung*, the Cologne paper Marx edited in 1842, gives us this description:

> Karl Marx from Trier was a powerful man of 24 whose thick black hair sprung from his cheeks, arms, nose, and ears. He was domineering, impetuous, passionate, full of boundless self-confidence, but at the same time deeply earnest and learned, a restless dialectician who with his restless Jewish penetration pushed every proposition of young Hegelian doctrine to its final conclusion.[20]

Aside from his "penetration" and his hairiness, Marx also sported a swarthy complexion which gave rise to his interesting alias.

Writes Engels, " 'The Moor' was Marx's nickname from his University days on. . . . If I had ever called him by some other name, he would have thought some misunderstanding had arisen between us."[21] Yet all his intimates understood "Moor" as "a veiled reminder of his Jewish origins." His daughter Eleanor undertook to lift the veil by learning Yiddish and "taking union" in the Jewish quarters of London. There, she was known to declare, "I am a Jewess"[22]—which was not literally true, since Jewish religious law counts descent through the mother. So vivid was her conviction of her beloved father's Jewishness that she freely took the identity on herself.

If modern writers on Marx leave his scurrilous attacks on Judaism unanswered, then, they run the risk of helping to perpetuate them. Along with Freud and Einstein, Marx is the modern world's figure of the Jew. Who should know better, the naive may justly ask, what Jewish faults are than the Jew Karl Marx?

II

Besides the moral obligation to combat antisemitism, there is another reason to be astonished at Marx scholars' neglect of the Jewish question, one that touches directly on their theoretical concerns. Let us say that Marx's real targets in this essay are the liberal notion of freedom and the modern separation of state and civil society as it is generally supposed. Marx achieves his commentary on these themes in a marvelously indirect manner. At every step of his argument, he makes his point by manipulating the various meanings he imputes to the symbol "Judaism" and by contrasting them with the meanings he ascribes to "Christianity." It would seem, then, that we have to unpack these heavily laden symbols in order to understand what Marx is saying about politics and freedom. But that is exactly what has not been done.

"The German Jews seek emancipation. What kind of emancipation do they want? *Civic, political* emancipation."[23] From his opening sentences on, Marx looks to the case of the Jews to shed light on how people become free. Bruno Bauer had argued that Judaism, with its arrogant peculiarity, prevented Jews from participating fully in the life of the state. If they would agree, for instance, to attend legislative session even when they took place on Saturday, then they would be eligible for the full set of rights that political emancipation implies.

> If, thereafter, some or many or *even the overwhelming majority felt obliged to fulfil their religious duties*, such practices should be left *to them as an absolutely* private matter.[24]

Precisely because it preserves religion as a private duty, Marx rejects political emancipation as an inadequate formula for human freedom. The Hegelian ideal of the state which motivates Bauer calls for politics to be a sphere of universality, in which all the higher needs of the spirit are met. To Bauer as well as to Marx himself, "the existence of religion is the existence of a defect."[25] If Jews (or Christians, for that matter) hold onto their religious practices, it is *prima facie* evidence that the state is not fulfilling their needs, and that the nonpolitical still exerts great power over their choices.

The incapacity of purely political means to make people free is not confined to the state's defeat by religion, however.

> The political elevation of man above religion shares the weaknesses and merits of all such political measures. For example, the state as a state abolishes *private property* (i.e., man decrees by *political* means the *abolition* of private property) when it abolishes the property *qualification* for electors and representatives. . . .
> But the political suppression of private property not only does not abolish private property, it actually presupposes its existence. The state abolishes, after its fashion, the distinctions established by *birth, social rank, education, occupation*, when it decrees that birth, social rank, education, occupation are *non-political* distinctions; when it proclaims, without regard to these distinctions, that every member of society is an *equal* partner in popular sovereignty, and treats all the elements which compose the real life of the nation from the standpoint of the state. But the state, nonetheless, allows private property, education, occupation, to *act* after *their* own fashion, namely as private property, education, occupation, and to manifest their *particular* nature.[26]

Instead of real universality, the state makes manifest "the illusory universality of modern political life."[27] Just as Jews do not become emancipated by the ballot if they still need the synagogue, so self-interested individuals do not become free, rational citizens simply by acquiring political rights. Both the Jew and the bourgeois remain subject to an external power, be it religion or money, even if (in their alienated way) they embrace it as their own. In fact, because politics has failed to create a home for the human spirit, the only sensible thing to do is to hang on to one's private good.

> Bauer asks the Jews: Have you, from your standpoint, the right to demand *political emancipation?* We ask the converse question: from the standpoint of *political* emancipation can the Jew be required to abolish Judaism, or man be asked to abolish religion?[28]

Remarkable is the sympathetic tone that Marx adopts toward his fellow Jews at this stage of the argument. It is almost as if he were cautioning them not to sell their birthright (on which he spends such harsh words later) for the mess of pottage that is modern citizenship. He reproves them, not for their religious faith, but for their political credulity.

> If you want to be politically emancipated, without emancipating yourselves humanly, the inadequacy and the contradiction is not entirely in yourselves but in the *nature* and the *category* of political emancipation. If you are preoccupied with this category you share the general prejudice.[29]

III

But of course, Marx does discover a real form of freedom for which he thinks giving up Judaism would be amply worthwhile: namely, "human emancipation." Oddly, in all the essay, he affords it only one paragraph of its own.

> Human emancipation will only be complete when the real, individual man has absorbed into himself the abstract citizen; when as an individual man, in his everyday life, in his work and in his relationships, he has become a *species-being;* and when he has recognized and organized his own powers (*forces propres*) as *social* powers so that he no longer separates this social power from himself as *political* power.[30]

This is an enigmatic passage, to say the least. It is difficult to tell what Marx means by "human emancipation," except that it will overcome the fragmentation and insufficiency of communal life that political emancipation only feeds. The problem for the reader is to discern that underlying the distinction between political and human emancipation is an even more basic divide: between "civil society" and the "political state." Or, to be even more precise, we need to realize that a society which splits life into these two spheres differs dramatically from a society in which they are united.

What is the "political state"? In the *Contribution to the Critique of Hegel's Philosophy of Right*, Marx traces the emergence of a sphere of politics, centered on government, laws, and constitutions, which lies alongside the parts of human life concerned with survival "without materially permeating the content of the remaining, non-political spheres." Hegel claimed that the state subsumed and transcended all the particular activities of material life. Marx debunks this claim of universality. As "political state," he argues, the state merely puts itself forth as one more fragment of national life, in no way integrating or integrated with the rest.

> In monarchy, for example, and in the republic as a merely particular form of state, political man has his particular mode of being alongside unpolitical man, man as a private individual. Property, contract, marriage, civil society, all appear here . . . as *particular* modes of existence alongside the political state, as the content to which the *political* state is related as *organizing* form; properly speaking, the relation of the political state to this content is merely that of reason, inherently without content, which defines and delimits, which now affirms and now denies.[31]

According to Marx, "the abstraction of *the state as such* belongs only to modern times, because the abstraction of private life belongs only to modern times." Other ages and other cultures did not split off the "political constitution as distinct from the material state of the other content of the life of the nation." In ancient Greece, for example, "the *res publica* is the real private affair of the citizens, their real content, and the private individual is a slave"—that is, *only* slaves bore the brand of an identity having nothing to do with their role in public life. During the Middle Ages, again, "the life of the nation and the life of the state are identical," but only because one's membership in an estate, a guild, or a corporation *determines* one's political status. "What distinguishes the modern state from these states characterized by the substantial unity between people and state," to Marx, is "that the constitution itself has been developed into a particular actuality alongside the life of the people—that the political state has become the constitution of the rest of the state."[32] The quest for a fully human existence is severed from, and set against, the activities which secure existence itself.

The same historical dividing up of social life that produces the political state at the same time gives birth to civil society. In "On the Jewish Question," Marx specifies that he means by civil society "the sphere of human needs, labour, private interests, and civil law."[33] From human needs, the other elements follow. Since Marx assesses human needs in two distinctly different ways, he also holds two opposed evaluations of civil society, neither of which, however, can stand without the other. Human needs are first of all for Marx a type of deprivation, an absence of something which frustrates human powers and stunts the development of the species. But at the same time, needs promote human invention, open up as yet unrealized capacities—in short, *spur* human development. Indeed, acquiring new and more sophisticated needs is part of what Marx thinks progress is all about.[34]

Civil society, the sphere of human needs, reflects both the negative and the positive evaluation of needs. Shorn of "even the *semblance* of a general content," civil society is a realm of pure egoism. Within it, each person is only "an individual separated from the community, withdrawn into himself, wholly preoccupied with his private interest and acting in accordance with his private caprice."[35] If the political state fails to provide universal freedom, civil society never aspires to it.

Paradoxically, then, Marx goes on to argue that civil society and not politics forms the real basis for human emancipation. "*Political* man is only abstract, artificial man, man as an *allegorical, moral* person."[36] Civil society, the world of practical need, constitutes the effective reality in which people actually live. Narrow and selfish it may be, but only changes in civil society can be powerful enough to move the species *beyond* civil society and political state alike, toward an integrated, meaningful, species life.

Both civil society and the political state are human inventions, as Marx sees it. Neither is natural or inevitable; both are becoming obsolete. Yet Marx champions the importance of civil society for future emancipation, not because it is good but because it is effective. His commitment embraces the nasty but real over the nice but fictional.

The dialectic between political state and civil society helps us to understand what Marx means by human, as opposed to merely political, emancipation. Political emancipation deepens the split in social life. Human emancipation overcomes it, reconstituting social relations on the basis of what people require in order both to survive and to live humanly. Without the concepts "civil society" and "political state," Marx's reply to Bauer seems perverse, or simply meaningless. Thus it is striking that no one has given a satisfying account of why Marx writes that the political state is "Christian," while civil society is "Jewish."[37]

Marx contradicts the liberal notion that separation of church and state removes politics from the influence of religion. Instead, he sees in liberal democracy "the perfected Christian state," more Christian even than "the Christian negation of the state." By privatizing religion instead of abolishing it, the political state helps perpetuate the Christian projection of human powers onto a transcendent God. In order to end this alienation, the state would have to become involved in answering the unmet needs that drive people to the solace of religion. Yet for the political state that is impossible, since (Marx argues) its whole claim to emancipate rests on its refusal to take private differences into account in the way it treats its citizens. There is neither rich nor poor, Jew nor Gentile, to the political state. For Marx, that fact alone speaks volumes about the origins of that state "under the sway of Christianity which *objectifies all* national, natural, moral, and theoretical relationships."[38]

We have already seen that Marx does not think any more highly of Judaism than of Christianity as a faith. Indeed, he tends to dismiss the content of Judaism altogether. How, then, can he identify civil society, the effective reality of social life, as "Jewish"? Marx draws a distinction between "sabbath" Judaism, the theology he considers an "insipid vapour," and "everyday" Judaism, "the particular situation of Judaism in the present enslaved world."[39] Just as civil society is the engine over which the political state draws a curtain, so the everyday Jew, in Marx's formulation, is the secret of the Jewish religion.

Marx sums up the Jewish situation in nineteenth-century Germany as "practical need, self-interest." Absent the economic discrimination they faced, the Jews would leave off being Jews: their burdens, he argues, define their identity. But "*practical need, egoism* is the principle of civil society" as well. For this reason, he asserts, "Judaism attains its apogee with the perfection of civil society; but civil society only reaches perfection in the *Christian* world." In other words, "Jewish" civil society only dominates the "Christian" political state once Christianity succeeds in separating the state from civil society. By attempting to banish human need, Christianity succumbs to it.

> It was only in appearance that Christianity overcame real Judaism. It was too *refined,* too spiritual to eliminate the crudeness of practical need except by raising it to the ethereal realm.[40]

IV

Reading what Marx has to say about Jews and Judaism as if it mattered enables us to make two interesting discoveries concerning the thinker and his theory. First, we learn that Marx's reputation as an antisemite obscures the true complexity of his views on Judaism. Judaism as a religion, he holds in greatest contempt. Judaism as a social power, on the other hand, Marx regards as supremely important. What Marx chooses to call "Jewish" is nothing less than the driving force of his social and political theory: the reality of human need, as expressed in the contradictions of capitalist society.

It is indeed no longer asked: which makes free—

> Judaism or Christianity? On the contrary, it is now asked: which makes free—the negation of Judaism or the negation of Christianity?[41]

Marx's answer is clear. The negation of "Judaism" is essential to emancipation, whereas the negation of "Christianity" leads to nothing—because the "Christian" political state is itself a nothing, an illusion possessed of no power to produce anything substantial. Marx's tribute to Judaism is the kind of recognition one grants a skilled and potent adversary. From a man who lists his idea of happiness as "to fight" and of misery "to submit," this is a compliment indeed.[42]

Against this reading, some might point to the language of the first of the "Theses on Feuerbach," where Marx charges that Feuerbach "regards the theoretical attitude as the only genuinely human attitude, while practice is conceived and fixed only in its dirty-judaical manifestation." I think this reference actually supports my interpretation. Marx is reproaching Feuerbach for regarding *all* practical activity as alienating—as, in "Jewish" civil society, it is. "Hence he does not grasp the significance of 'revolutionary,' of practical-critical activity."[43]

Marx's point here is that Feuerbach holds a prejudice against practice which parallels the prejudice against Jews. In both cases, he counsels, one must look objectively to the contradictions embodied in each to see them as signs of a potentially progressive future. This escapes Feuerbach, whose "materialism" degenerates into a blind faith in the empirical present.

As a corollary, we must realize that we have not understood what Marx's theory means until we understand what Judaism means to Marx. We know that it symbolizes the gritty details of how people make a living, the historically unsolved problem of human need. But why *this* symbol?[44] Such representations do not, as a rule, arise from nowhere: they are prepared by associations in the writer's mind which grow more vivid at opportune moments, only to fade when they begin no longer to be needed. Jerrold Seigel points out one reason why Judaism may have seemed particularly relevant to Marx in 1843—his opponent.

> If Bauer was a former religious Christian who had freed himself by denying Christianity, Marx was in origin a secularized Jew who regarded himself as liberated from "practical Judaism," self-interest. Marx's claim against Bauer was that his own personal standpoint—granting all its defects—rather than Bauer's, provided the point of entry for true human liberation.[45]

Certainly, there is something to this. Bauer's argument and Marx's reply resemble nothing so much as a religious disputation. Like the Christian clerics, Bauer claims Judaism has outlived its reason for being and only survives on invincible, stubborn refusal to see the facts. Marx argues like a rabbi who is mindful of the monarch's eye: without claiming any positive virtues for the faith, he finds reasons nonetheless to justify its existence, and thus bests his accuser at his own game.[46] While this desire to score points on Bauer may tell us something about Marx's motivation, it still leaves the content of Marx's symbolic use of "Judaism" wholly unexplained.

Our reading of this essay therefore leads us to ask yet a third question: the "Jewish question" itself. What did nineteenth-century Germans mean by "the Jewish question"? What did the phrase mean to Marx? What was Marx's own experience of Jews and Judaism outside his immediate family, and how did it color what he had to say on the issue? If the "Jewish question" is tied up in Marx's mind with his ideas about how people become free, then what does his stance toward the emancipation of the Jews tell us about his notion of freedom?

At the beginning of the nineteenth century, when German liberals inspired by French revolutionary ideals were agitating the Prussian monarchy for a constitution, the status of Jews throughout the kingdom was no different from what it had been during the Middle Ages. Jews were not citizens in Germany. Under the law, they were not even human. They existed as *servi camerae*, "serfs of the chamber," the personal property of the king to be disposed of at his pleasure. German rulers valued their Jews as an unending source of revenue. They zealously maintained the autonomous Jewish social structure so as to make entire Jewish communities responsible for tax levies collectively. Nonpayment was likely to result in the taking of the rabbi or other local leaders as hostages.

Like other serfs, Jews could not move from one town to another, marry, or have more than one child without permission. Because of their international connections, however, Jews were officially encouraged to settle in Germany with a view to facilitating trade. Periodically, to assuage Christian merchants' resentment, the government turned a blind eye while pogroms, anti-Jewish riots, decimated the Jewish population. Invariably, after violence had died down, a new set of Jews would be invited to continue the cycle.[47]

Under Napoleon, after a lengthy investigation of their allegiance, the Jews of Germany became citizens before the law. In practice, the edict was enforced spottily. Because of its origins, Jewish emancipation "was stigmatized by the concept of tyranny which in the eyes of the gentile population was attached to all acts of the Napoleonic regime."[48] The year 1816 saw the restrictions on Jewish trade which aroused Heschel Marx's protest; in 1817, the decrees against Jewish lawyers moved him to convert. In the year Karl Marx was born, anti-Jewish riots broke out in Prussia and continued into the next year. (Because some Jews, especially veterans of the Napoleonic wars, fought back, the whole Jewish community of Wurzburg was expelled.)[49] In December 1822, Frederick William III barred Jews from teaching at universities or schools.[50] The advocates of Jewish emancipation were forced to realize that nominal citizenship would not suffice. They turned their efforts to tearing down all invidious legislation standing in the way of full Jewish participation in public life.

However, before they could grapple with the laws, they had to confront centuries-old prejudices against the Jewish people. "The image of the Jew prevailing in the public mind," writes leading historian Jacob Katz,

> was the image of the popular Christian tradition, combining the theological tenets of the Jews' guilt in rejecting the Christian message and an aversion to the foreign tradesmen whose greed and cunning remain unchecked by a common brotherhood in the one creed.[51]

That this caricature convinced many educated Germans is borne out in the history of the term "Jewish emancipation." The Jews' initial thrust at citizenship was called "naturalization," implying that all Jews had been aliens in Germany up until then. An enlightened Protestant minister then introduced the nomenclature "civic betterment" (*burgerliche verbesserung*), which became widespread, partly because it left ambiguous who was to be bettered, society or the Jews. (The term "advancement" in the name of the National Association for the Advancement of Colored People shares some of the same uncertainty.) Jewish advocates finally took up the term "emancipation" because it "implied that natural rights had been withheld till then from those concerned, and that these must be restored to them unconditionally."[52] Precisely for this reason, opponents of Jewish rights objected strenuously to the label "emancipation." Jews, they contended, already had all the rights they could handle: as Jews they were too morally degraded to be equal to full citizenship.[53]

The fear and suspicion of Jews that led to denunciations such as these did not arise only from the popular images of Christ-killers and Jewish moneymen. Cultural differences made the Jews and Christians of Europe strangers to each other, all the more incomprehensible for their apparent similarities. From the Christian side, the "Jewish question" took on the form of the query, "Are the Jews congenitally unsociable and rude, or are they this way as the result of being segregated into ghettos?" John Murray Cuddihy calls this emphasis on the unseemly manners of the would-be emancipated Jews "the ordeal of civility." "This problem," he writes, "stems ultimately . . . from a disabling inability of Judaism to legitimate culturally the differentiation of culture and society."[54] Put more simply: the Jews of Europe could not, would not, or failed to recognize the need to privatize their particular concerns and characteristics in order to become good citizens.

The politeness of public life in the Christian polity, "the fragile solidarity of the surface we call civility," created a schism in the lives and the personalities of the Jews who first encountered it.

> With the advent of Jewish emancipation, when ghetto walls crumble and the *shtetlach* begin to dissolve, Jewry—like some wide-eyed anthropologist—enters upon a strange world, to explore a strange people observing a strange *halakha* [code of conduct]. They examine this world in dismay, with wonder, anger, and punitive objectivity.[55]

The Christian world, of course, returns the compliment, judging Jewish behavior by its own standards as "public misconduct," and resisting every attempt to violate its norms of what can be spoken of and what, for the sake of decency, must be kept silent.

The Jewish question in Germany, then, was nothing else but Christian puzzlement as to how to treat an entire people who are unfitted to be free. Now, although Marx rejects its theological underpinnings, he shares the common assessment of the Jewish religion. Indeed, his strictures on "Jewish Jesuitism" descend in a straight line from the gospel image of the Pharisees via Paul's anathema on "the Law" in the name of "the Spirit."[56] About the provenance of this stereotype, at least, there is no mystery. Marx also accepts the stock picture of the Jewish moneyman, right down to the term *Judentum* for "commerce." Even if he does twist its usual meaning into an indictment of Christian society for its own "Jewishness," he can only achieve this end by agreeing to identify Jews with money.

Neither Marx nor his Left Hegelian contemporaries saw anything extraordinary in this equation. Bruno Bauer writes in *Die Judenfrage* that the Jews are a parasite nation who live beyond their appointed era by usury: they contribute nothing productive to Christian society.[57] Ludwig Feuerbach goes even further. In *The Essence of Christianity,* in words that Marx would echo, he states that the Jewish god is "the most practical principle in the world—namely, egoism; and moreover egoism in the form of religion. Egoism is the God who will not let his servants come to shame." Furthermore, he accuses the Jews of "the alimentary view of theology."

> Eating is the most solemn act or the initiation of the Jewish religion. In eating, the Israelite celebrates and renews the act of creation; in eating man declares Nature to be an insignificant object. When the seventy elders ascended the mountain with Moses, "they saw God; and when they had seen God they ate and drank." Thus with them what the sight of the Supreme Being heightened was the appetite for food.[58]

As Marx Wartofsky pointed out, when Feuerbach discusses Holy Communion, he sees nothing gross or ignoble in the act of eating: "On the contrary, it is seen as man's ennoblement of his dependence on water, wine, and bread, as the stuff of life."[59] But when Feuerbach's subject is the Jews, he loses no opportunity to stress their selfishness, materialism, and absurd practicality. Marx sees a social meaning in Jewish egoism where Feuerbach does not, but they both agree that Jews are egoists as long as they are Jews.

What is curious about this is that nothing in Marx's native milieu would naturally lead him to this conclusion. His birthplace, Trier, contained only 260 Jews out of a population of 12,000—a little higher than the national average, but still only roughly 2 percent. Among the more urban of the Jews of Trier, the most widespread occupations were artisanship and innkeeping, not moneylending or trade. There was little scope for high finance in Trier anyway. Located in the heart of the Moselle wine country, its economy was primarily agricultural. In fact, although a higher percentage of Jews than non-Jews lived in cities, the Jewish population of the government district centered on Trier was 68.5 percent rural—more than two-thirds.[60] If Marx had written only of what he really experienced, neither his negative identification of Jews and "huckstering," nor its double, Judaism as the elemental social force of human need, would have been possible for him.

V

The symbols "Jew" and "Judaism" in Karl Marx's "On the Jewish Question" owe their existence to widely held stereotypes rather than empirical example. Marx employs them as literary terms of art, playing on their various nuances to denigrate the political state (because its existence implies that of "Jewish" civil society), and to assert the superiority of his own approach ("the negation of Judaism") to the problem of how to make humanity free.

Having said this, we still must wonder exactly what Marx meant by "Judaism." For, within the boundaries of those stereotypes, there is simply no room for the positive connotations that the association with practical need sheds on Judaism in Marx's theory. Instead of ennobling Judaism, one would think that the connection with casuistry, greed, and outlandish manners would demean civil society. Yet for Marx, although the "Jewishness" of civil society is an argument for transcending it, its "Jewish" character is what makes its transcendence (and that of the state, and of the rift between them) possible. Apparently, the Jewish defects of civil society are its virtues as well. How can we understand this?

We must remember our earlier observation that for Marx to place value on any social phenomenon, it must really exist, that is, produce material effects. (Marx's view is no simple utilitarianism: effective reality is a necessary condition of his esteem, but not always sufficient.) By this standard, we can readily see that

"Jewish rudeness" must indeed be judged a virtue. In "On the Jewish Question," as noted earlier, Marx declares Christianity "too *refined*, too spiritual to eliminate the crudeness of practical need."[61] It takes no great leap of the imagination to read this as an indirect swipe at Bruno Bauer, since ignoring the power of practical need over political life is Marx's precise reproach to his former teacher. By calling attention to the brute economic facts, Marx violates the norms of Left Hegelian discourse and states unwelcome truths in an obnoxious "Jewish" manner.

Nor does he let the matter rest. In *The Holy Family*, the interminable polemic against the Left Hegelian "Critical Critics" that Marx and Engels compiled in 1844, the authors attack "St. Bruno" once again. And once more, Marx chooses the Jewish question as his battlefield. This time, however, he draws a tight connection between Jewish vulgarism and the ability to see the meaning of real human freedom, the kind that only communism (he now asserts) can achieve.

> To the massy, material Jews is to be preached the *Christian* doctrine of *spiritual freedom*, of *freedom in theory*, that *spiritualistic* freedom that *imagines* itself to be free even in chains, that is blissful in "*the idea*" and that is only embarrassed by all massy existence. . . . From this statement one can measure at once the critical cleavage that divides *massy*, profane socialism and communism from *absolute* socialism. The first principle of profane socialism rejects emancipation *in mere theory* as an illusion, and desires for *real* freedom, besides the idealistic "*will*," very palpable, material conditions.[62]

The Jews are "massy" (of the masses, plebian) and they lead a "massy existence" (lumpish, material, real). They cannot imagine real freedom on their own: that is left for Marx himself to do. Nevertheless, even they are capable of seeing that Bauer's proffered form of freedom stems partly from the desire not to be "embarrassed" by them any longer. For their cramped but secure mode of survival, Bauer offers "emancipation *in mere theory*." We can hear Marx warning, as he did in "On the Jewish Question," that the Jews must hold out for the real thing.

Even more, however, we can recognize an unexpected parallel Marx is drawing between profane socialism and the Jews. Profane socialism, in fact, seemed to be distinguished by its insistence on changing "very palpable, material conditions": the same program which, one year earlier, Marx had called "the negation [or abolition, or transcendence] of Judaism." Marx's success at coming to grips with the real issue (as he understood it) of human freedom is here connected, not with his education, or with his class background, but with his Jewishness. In later works, he tries to dodge the issue of his own consciousness, but here, between the lines, he hints at an explanation.

When we consider the argument of *The Holy Family* in conjunction with the line Marx pursues in "On the Jewish Question," the example of the Jews shows us vital elements of how Marx believes people become free. One predisposing factor is certainly the position they occupy in civil society, or what Marx calls "the particular situation of Judaism in the present enslaved world."[63] Another such factor would be a standpoint which is not "too *refined*, too spiritual," to concede the vicissitudes of human need; a perspective, a set of cultural resources that direct people to take material conditions seriously without being cowed into accepting them as immutable. Over his lifetime, Marx oscillates between granting one or the other the primary role. When revolution looks imminent, he credits objective social relations, while when the prospects of upheaval dim, he turns to blame the ideological limitations of the masses.[64] But in general, his attention shifts to the study of political economy, and as it does, the proletariat takes center stage, while the Jews disappear into the wings.

Continuously throughout Marx's writings, however, we find in his notion of freedom a tension that appears first and most clearly in "On the Jewish Question" as we have read it. Everyday, practical Judaism is rooted, according to Marx, in the realities of civil society during a capitalistic age. For that reason, its negation goes lockstep with the superseding of the conditions that maintain it: the power of money; the exchange system; ultimately, capitalism itself. In the freed world, the Jewish perspective which has criticized the old society and helped the new one to be born would lose its reason for being. Both in its sabbath and everyday versions, it would disappear: the former exploded, the latter deprived of its material basis. The "particular situation" of Judaism would be dissolved. The Jews themselves would be absorbed into the species as the abstract citizen is absorbed into the individual.

And yet . . . even from the standpoint of *human* emancipation, "can the Jews be required to abolish Judaism?" Emancipation, as Marx describes it, proceeds by reading one's "particular situation" closely, finding its hidden possibilities, and reinterpreting it through action in order to become its author. It cannot succeed, however, if in the rereading, the author is annihilated—for then who is it that becomes free? Marx's own identity is bound up with the "Jewish" activity of criticizing alienated human life. In what possible world would his anxiety over trading the substantial Jewish perspective for an illusory freedom finally disappear?

All of which presents us with a fourth and final question about Karl Marx. Could it be that Marx's social and political theory in general is structured by assumptions and patterns of thought which can also be found within the Jewish tradition? How would recognizing these affinities have transformed Marx's understanding of his theory? How might it affect ours?

This is the Jewish question about Marx we will explore in the following chapters.

The Power
of the Tongue

Are we Jews? Are we Greeks? We live in the difference between
the Jew and the Greek, which is perhaps the unity of what is
called history. We live in and of difference; that is, in hypoc-
risy. . . .

Are we Greeks? Are we Jews? But what are we? Are we (not a
chronological, but a prelogical question) *first* Jews or *first*
Greeks? And does the strange dialogue between the Jew and the
Greek, peace itself, have the form of the absolute speculative
logic of Hegel, the living logic which *reconciles* formal tautology
and empirical heterology. . . . Or, on the contrary, does this peace
have the form of infinite separation and of the unthinkable, un-
sayable transcendence of the other? To what horizon of peace
does the language which asks this question belong? From
whence does it draw the energy of its question? Can it account
for the historical *coupling* of Judaism and Hellenism? And what
is the legitimacy, what is the meaning of the *copula* in this proposition from perhaps the most Hegelian of modern novelists:
"Jewgreek is greekjew. Extremes meet."?—Jacques Derrida, "Violence and Metaphysics"[1]

THE TRADITION within which theorists generally
read the writings of Marx is called "modern political thought." It
is a philosophical family tree that stretches from Machiavelli
down to the present day. Modern political thought traces its roots
back to medieval Christian theology, and whether by continuing
it or by reacting against it, modern theorists acknowledge this
inheritance. Because of its Christian roots, much of modern
political thought has nurtured itself on a distinctive understanding of reality—what philosophers generally call an ontology. This
ontology rests on the attempt to combine Jewish thinking with

Greek thinking which has characterized much of Christian theology.

Derrida's pointed questions suggest, however, that neither the theological nor the theoretical enterprise squarely confronts the question of its own possibility. What if Jewish and Greek thinking were radically and irreconcilably different, and to synthesize them would be to do violence to both? In order to consider that possibility, theorists and theologians alike would have to renounce their dream of absolute knowledge, whether of the world or the cosmos. We could fit the way things are into one clear picture only if, from the right perspective, the whole of reality made a single sense. If, however, the ontology on which moderns have relied were fundamentally in tension with itself, then truth would speak in many voices, and it would have to be heard that way, as well.

Derrida argues that, faced with a bedrock conflict between Jew and Greek, theorists should feel enormous pressure to question their motives for doing theory. What interest, he asks, compels the enforced détente between the two modes of thought? Why do we cry "peace, peace" when there is no peace? In the reduction of two divergent species of thought to one and the same—and, most keenly, in the expulsion of the specifically Jewish, and the consequent bodily immersion of Western thought in the baptismal waters of the Greco-Christian tradition—Derrida detects a kind of Inquisition. He opposes this "ontological, or transcendental oppression,"[2] which does not consist of imposing one ontology on another but rather of posing "ontology" (reality as Being, a peculiarly Greek notion) as the only way reality can be understood.[3]

Whether or not we confirm the full range of Derrida's suspicions, we find that simply in order to ask whether Jewish patterns of thought reemerge in Karl Marx's thinking, we shall have to rescue from disuse the difference between Jew and Greek in modern political theory. By itself, however, that will hardly suffice. If modern political thought does indeed move within the "horizon of peace" of which Derrida speaks, if we are trained to expect conflicting views to melt into one underlying truth or never to meet at all, then we should expect to find it hard to grasp the real, stubborn difference between the two. Jewish and Greek modes of thought are not "entirely discrete functions that can be neatly peeled apart for inspection—apparently, like the different colored strands of electrical wiring."[4] Especially for a thinker like Marx, who stands in ambiguous relation *both* to Judaism and to Greek philosophy, the illusory unity that philosophical language forges out of the two traditions becomes an inescapable feature of linguistic reality. The enforced identity of the two traditions sets limits to what a thinker can say, write, or even think, if he or she means to be intelligible.

So, "theory itself becomes a material force," as Marx once put it, in an entirely unexpected way.[5] The modern theoretical practice of collapsing Jewish assumptions about reality into Greek ontology insures that Marx, writing as a theorist, will exhibit neither in any unalloyed form. We would be mistaken to look for pure samples of either in his writings.

How, then, can we go about inquiring into the affinities between Marx's ontology and traditional Jewish thought, if comparing them directly is only a first step? I propose we use the special hermeneutic style characterized earlier as a non-"Marxist" reading of Marx: to seek out gaps, discrepancies, rough spots, incipient contradictions in Marx's ontology, and to read through and beyond them to understand what that thought now means.

In the following discussion, then, we shall be concerned with the incapacity of more orthodox readers of Marx, grounding themselves in the Greco-Christian tradition, to reach all of the complexities of the real that Marx either displays or presupposes. Where they fall short, we will investigate whether placing Marx's theory in the context of Jewish thought gives a more satisfying account.

We can employ the method of interpreting the gaps in Marx's writings that a Greek-oriented reading leaves unnoticed even if we suspect that the first one to read them that way was Marx himself. The philosophy of writing we identified earlier as Marx's does not allow him the luxury of being the final arbiter of his own meaning. Respectfully, we may dispute his self-interpretation. Indeed, respect may demand that we do so. If, in the process of searching out the hidden implications of his understanding of reality, we find affinities with Jewish thought, refracted though they may be, we will then have reason to question Marx's inattention to the relation between Judaism and his own thinking. From examining the interstices of his writing, we would then turn to probing the curious absences in his life and thought, adding another, less obvious dimension to the Jewish question about Marx.

But let us turn first to exploring exactly how Jewish and Greek thought diverge, and where they lead.

I

> Life and death are in the power of the tongue.
> —Babylonian Talmud[6]

While its exact nature has been the subject of lively dispute, the contrast between "Greek" and "Hebrew" modes of thought has flourished in the West for centuries. Matthew Arnold, in a famous essay, declared, "Hebraism and Hellenism—between these two points of influence moves our world."[7] In the earlier part of the twentieth century, with his magisterial *Israel: Its Life and Culture,* Johannes Pedersen devoted four volumes to a historical examination which presumes and reinforces this contrast.[8] The classic exposition, however, arrives with Thorleif Boman's *Hebrew Thought Compared with Greek.* Despite severe criticism, some of it justified, this work remains the indispensable starting point for discussion of Jewish and Greek thinking. To see how the contrast has been drawn, therefore, we will go into it in some detail.

Boman portrays Hebrew and Greek thought as diametrically opposed views of reality. A Greek would find Hebrew thinking strange, and a Hebrew thinker would find Greek thought foreign. The difference between the two is systematic: "It does not lie in any [one] word or in a circumscribed viewpoint; yet it extends throughout the whole to every detail." The opposition between Hebrew and Greek applies not only to thought, but also to feeling and judgment, too. Interesting, in light of our earlier finding that "rudeness" made the emancipation of European Jews impractical, is Boman's following observation:

From [its own] viewpoint Greek mental activity appears harmonious, prudent, moderate, and peaceful; to the person to whom
Greek kind of thinking occurs plainly as ideal, Hebrew thinking
and its manners of expression appear exaggerated, immoderate,
discordant, and in bad taste.[9]

What divides these two great cultural styles so sharply? In the
first place, it is their ontology, in the strict sense of "notion of
being." Boman describes Greek ontology as static—or, in its own
terms, harmonious. What really is, for the Greeks, always is.

All being is therefore at rest and in harmony, and all higher being is
unalterable and indestructible; there is also a certain order of rank
among all existing things. The more original a thing is, the more
being it has and the higher is its dignity.

Examples spring to mind of how Greek philosophers constantly
presume that what changes or passes away is not as real, true, or
good as what remains fixed and unmoving. In the *Timaeus*, Plato
assigns the creation of the world to a lesser divinity, or demiurge,
carefully keeping the ultimate persona of his god above the process, as if action and material substance were media too gross for
the highest reality. In the *Symposium,* he discusses how human
love can become divine by ascending gradually from the inciden-
tal beauty of an individual to the idea of beauty itself, which never
alters.[10] The whole Platonic doctrine of the forms emphasizes
that true being manifests itself only imperfectly, as shadows on
the walls of a dimly lit cave, as long as it must inhabit physical
bodies. Bodies age and decay, matter crumbles, but reality is
eternal.

For Boman, the Greek conception of the world reaches its full-
est expression in the works of Plato, so that he treats Aristotle
primarily as a later Platonist. This is problematic. Aristotle's teleology, or doctrine of final ends, stretches the "order of rank
among all existing things" over time, so that in his philosophy,
any being may eventually reach the peculiar excellence of which it
is capable. In addition, the idea of a *telos*—as opposed to that of
an *eidos*, or form—lifts some of the stigma of mortality from
bodily human existence. The notion of teleological development
allows for the human life cycle; it even sets a value on growth and
change, as long as they conduce to the final end. In light of this,

Western theory has celebrated Plato as the philosopher of being and Aristotle as the philosopher of becoming.

In Boman's view and by comparison with Hebrew thought, however, Aristotle's conception hardly seems such a great departure. Plato's "forms" set a standard for the good life which is given before any and all attempts to live it. Aristotle's "ends" and "excellence" do the same. Neither thinker permits human beings to determine (or take part in determining) our own goals: we are only to discover them and to embody them, as far as we are able. In this manner, Boman implies, Aristotle's ontology, like Plato's, rests on the disposition to regard reality and the human role within as essentially fixed.[11]

Very consistently, therefore, Aristotle reserves his highest ethical rung for the followers of the contemplative life, who fix their attention on the immutable truths that the universe displays for the edification of human reason.[12] In the Greek tradition, spiritual realities befit the concern of the most noble persons, and the saintliest souls are those who devote their lives to those things they cannot change.

Boman's reading will, of course, outrage the sensibilities of anyone accustomed to thinking of Plato and Aristotle as the opposite poles of Western thought. In *The Fragility of Goodness*, Martha Nussbaum provides that point of view with a new foundation.[13] Greek thought, in her view, is fundamentally about tragic choices and the real power of events over our ability to lead praiseworthy lives. Plato, she argues, tries to eliminate the power of luck; Aristotle and the Greek tragedians aim to teach us how to yield to it nobly. Plato's ambition to create a rational world fits the equation of "Greek" with "static," but Aristotle's practical attempt to live a balanced life does not.

Nussbaum's interpretation is compelling precisely because it reveals a dimension of Greek thought we rarely encounter today. As her own sources show, the Aristotle we meet in contemporary discussions is a Baconian scientist making empirical observations, not the subtle interpreter of culture she portrays.[14] Before that, from the Middle Ages to the Enlightenment, Aristotle was "the Philosopher," the voice of reason, second only to the Bible as an unquestioned authority.[15]

Boman's characterization of Greek thought seems to rest on these older views of Aristotle, not on Nussbaum's perception of him. It depends on one's perspective: from Jerusalem, the distance between Athens and Scythia may look very small, and the view from Jerusalem is what most concerns us here. Besides, like most philosophers, Aristotle looks different depending on which of his concerns we emphasize. If we stress his attention to cultural practices and prudent reasoning, he may offer a more active alternative to Plato's world of forms; when we recall his endless categorization and his ethical insistence on the golden mean, his world once again seems to have a place for everything and everything in its place.

For the Hebrew thinker of biblical times, in contrast, reality is dynamic and constantly in motion. Boman states: "Motionless and fixed being is for the Hebrews a nonentity; it does not exist for them."[16] What is, to the Hebrew mind, is *not* always the same: it moves, it changes, it acts and responds to actions.

To illustrate this proposition, Boman points to various peculiarities of the way that verbs function in the Hebrew language. "To be" and "to become" are the same word in Hebrew, and that word, *hayah,* is "a true verb with full verbal force."[17] Through countless examples, Boman demonstrates that *hayah* virtually always means action—the producing of an effect. Consequently, the idea of ontology as "study of being" misleads us when we examine that which is real to Hebrew thought. In biblical usage, insofar as "being" is something real, it is also "becoming," while being as distinct from becoming hardly seems real at all: the two are fused.

Boman provides a further example of the dynamism of biblical Hebrew—its verb tenses. Modern Hebrew follows the pattern English-speaking people know best. It divides all actions into past, present, and future. The Bible, however, knows but two tenses: perfect and imperfect. The first designates action which has reached its completion; the second refers to action, the effects of which are "still in process of coming and becoming."[18] Hebrew thought treats continuity and change as one; similarly, Boman understands it to consider actions together with their lived consequences. As long as a deed continues to make its influence felt on the course of current events, it is present and incomplete.

Whether an action has reached its fullness does not depend on the essential qualities of the activity, or on the detached judgment of some hypothetical observer. Rather, it is determined by how the act resonates in the life of someone caught up in the process which it sets into motion. Therefore, it is entirely possible for different people to view the same situation as ended or not yet complete, depending on their relation to it and their motive for categorizing it. Thus, the structure of Hebrew verb tenses moves the Hebraically minded thinker to think of reality as only partly formed and still pliable, yet capable of imposing an obligation to act. Reality may even manifest itself most strikingly where it is most incomplete, since that is where it most demands action. The Hebrew universe is not only dynamic but relational, as well.

Because it organizes reality "from the standpoint of an experiencing person," Hebrew thought identifies time with the events it contains, while Greek thinking, in order to come to grips with time at all, must express it in terms of space. Consider the time line, a conceptual device that maps our complex and often confused sense of time's passage onto the physical distance between one point and another. Boman traces the origin of the spatial metaphor to Plato's definition of time as "a moving image of eternity" and Aristotle's claim that temporal existence is best represented "by the image of movement along a line."[19]

A line is infinitely thin, because each of its points occupies no area. It stretches on to infinity in both directions simply by juxtaposing points; it never relates them one to the next, or melds them into any large entity. What matters for this conceptualization is not *what kind* of time one passes but simply *how much*. Amounts of time, in turn, come to be gauged according to the language of distance, by *how far* one "point in time" lies from another.

In contrast to this formal and quantitative approach to time, Boman explains, "the Israelites understand time as something qualitative, because for them time is determined by its content." Events mark time's passage, engraving specific moments in memory. Of course, Hebrew thinkers can still tell noon from midnight, or one year from another. But far more important are the expressions which do not merely define a period for us but actually acquaint us with it: "wartime, peacetime, hard times, time of mourning, feast time, favourable time." Biblical Hebrew discerns an intrinsic connection between times and activities, as in the famous verse from Ecclesiastes, "To everything there is a season, and a time for every purpose under heaven: a time to be born and a time to die."[20] The purposes of particular moments come to relate them to each other, so that eventually, time is mediated through the life experience of societies and individuals.

Because Hebrew thought perceives different occasions as internally related rather than as mere "points in time," Boman believes it immensely advances "the capacity for experiencing contemporaneity."[21] Historian Yosef Hayim Yerushalmi has observed that up until the modern era, Jews hardly relied at all on the writing of history to preserve group memories. Instead, in evocative ceremonies like the Passover Seder, "both the language and the gesture are designed to spur, not so much a leap of memory as a fusion of past and present. Memory here is no longer recollection, which still preserves a sense of distance, but reactualization."[22]

What makes different historical moments contemporaneous to the Hebraic thinker is their import for the fulfillment of divine commands. Just as individual and social purposes structure the human sense of time in everyday life, so does Boman think God's purposes (as they understand them) organize the Hebrews' understanding of history. "Hence in the framework of Hebrew piety eschatology is just as necessary a conclusion as immutable eternity is for the Greeks who think religiously."[23]

For the Greeks, who want to know how things really are, there is a huge difference between form and content, and form—the more general, stable category—is reality at its highest. Hebrews, according to Boman, refuse to separate form from content, spirit from matter. They manage to make comparisons and draw distinctions without resorting to formal definition.

When we [sic] draw a tree-trunk, we first of all draw the outline with two vertical lines; we believe that we can even see the contour. We are really in error, however, for when we go up to the tree and go around it, we can only see bark and wood, but no kind of strokes, lines, or contours. Thus, these are only auxiliary lines which we introduce voluntarily into what we see in order to make a representation of the visual impression. . . . According to certain techniques we can suppress our natural tendency and see, draw, and paint the object without contours. This is precisely what the Israelites do by nature.[24]

The correctness of Boman's art theory is not at issue here. His point is evident: drawing lines around reality may not finally depict it any more clearly. Boman notes that the word "definition" comes from the Latin *findo*, or "split." "If a piece of wood is split into two parts, and they are put back together, there is a boundary line between the two pieces, a line which takes up no space." So, too, Greek thinkers abstract from matter to create abstract representations which, unlike real objects, can be defined by drawing boundaries. "It is in such acts as these that Greek, Indo-European logical thinking consists."[25] (Here, Aristotle even more than Plato exemplifies Greek thought.)

Hebrew thinking, by the same token, is like perception without auxiliary lines: at its sharpest at the center of its field of vision, it "diminishes in clarity in all directions until it ends in imperceptibility."[26] To "define" something in this mode is to progress from its clear, paradoxically definitive center in one's own experience of it toward the fringes of one's relation to it.

Three other contrasts between Hebrew and Greek thought fit the overall pattern: disagreements on the relation between thought and thing, on that of word and deed, and on the nature of truth. On the one hand, to the Greek mind, "the thing is a means of knowing. The one who seeks to know is not attempting to alter something or other in his environment, but he is trying only to observe how it really is." To reflect on true being is to partake of the divine: indeed, "the standpoint of the spectator is already divine in itself." To the Hebrew, however, "things have a meaning; they are symbols given in nature."[27] A Hebrew thinker would fail utterly to comprehend Goethe's epigram, "all that is transitory is only a symbol," because seeking to find a guide to action in the fleeting events of life is paying attention to precisely what is real, from the biblical standpoint.[28]

Likewise, where the Greek philosophers complain of the inadequacy of language, to the Hebrew thinker, true speech is synonymous with effective reality. One term, *davar*, covers the meanings *thing, word,* and *matter.* "A lie for the Hebrew is not as it is for us [*sic*] a nonagreement with the truth. For him, the lie is the internal decay and destruction of the word." Language has power, and truth is the word's result in action. "That which is powerless, empty, and vain is a lie: a spring which gives no water lies."[29] Hebrew thought accordingly seeks truth in trustworthy relations between actors in the temporal and material world, while Greek thought looks for truth in valid perceptions of the eternal, spiritual reality.

The distinction could not be more clear—but it must become much more precise before we can inquire where, in its terms, the thinking of Karl Marx stands.

II

Boman's comparison of Hebrew and Greek thought makes very strong claims on the basis of language, and it has drawn criticism of equal intensity from those who study linguistics. James Barr attacks, not the "thought contrast" itself, but the semantic method supporting it, on three main grounds. First, he argues, Boman's survey of Hebrew and Greek is unsystematic.[30] Second, he raises serious doubts about whether language and thought directly correlate, as Boman constantly presumes.[31] Barr warns of "the danger of taking a sense of a word along with its context and suggesting that the significance which is given through associations of the context is in fact the indicator value of the word."[32] Not all particularities of a language tell us anything about the way the speakers of that language think.[33] Barr explains:

> Even on the most general theoretical level, if a relation is assumed to exist between the mental pattern of a certain linguistic group and the structure of their language, one would have the choice of at least the following simple relations: a) that the mental pattern is determined by the linguistic structure; b) that the linguistic structure is determined by the mental pattern; c) that they are in some way reciprocally interactive. Under c) can perhaps be added the further alternative d) that the interaction is not constant and uniform, but occurs only haphazardly and at certain points and therefore for reasons and circumstances which have to be separately determined in each case.[34]

Finally, Barr attributes to Boman a vested interest in the Hebrew-Greek distinction arising out of the desire to prove "the uniqueness of Christianity," which is supposed to be their reconciliation.[35]

These criticisms and cautions serve the useful purpose of alerting us when Boman's enthusiasm for his subject carries him away. We can explain these excesses by recognizing Boman's very Greek approach to distinguishing Greek from Hebrew thought. When Boman contrasts the two modes, he draws lines of demarcation between them, "defining" them by mutual exclusion after the fashion he calls in others "Indo-European logical thinking."[36] Taking the identifying marks as the modes themselves, he reinvents Hebrew and Greek as abstract types. He can then construe the examples he cites as the matter that embodies the formal categories, and this makes easy the overinterpretation of which Barr complains.

Beyond that, Boman's typology fails to allow for historical change. His concepts "Hebrew" and "Greek" reside in some timeless and universal dimension of thought, as in reality languages can do only when they are dead. Boman locates the two modes within a world of ideas and thinkers in which Hebrew and Greek exist as opposing essences, always have, and always will, even (one suspects) if there had never been any Jews or Greeks to instantiate them. Consequently, he lays himself open to Barr's methodological reproach.

But where Boman overestimates his ability to think Hebraically, Barr makes no effort at all in that direction. For him, whether Greek thought differs from Hebrew can *only* be settled through Greek-like processes of definition and exclusion. To Barr, for instance, the meaning of a word properly consists of its "indicator value," a kind of Platonic ideal of the word that transcends any particular context in which it visibly appears. The Hebraic suggestion that proper meaning might actually be constituted by context would seem to him absurd. Barr, therefore, stands in the uncomfortable position of Alice beyond the looking glass, in the Red Queen's garden.

"When you say 'hill,'" the Queen interrupted, "I could show you hills, in comparison with which you'd call that a valley."

"No, I shouldn't," said Alice, surprised into contradicting her at last: "a hill *can't* be a valley, you know. That would be nonsense—"

> The Red Queen shook her head. "You may call it 'nonsense' if you like," she said, "but *I've* heard nonsense, compared with which that would be as sensible as a dictionary!"[37]

The Red Queen, infuriating though she may be, has it exactly right. To a mind which, like Barr's, conceives truth as never varying regardless of persons, a hill cannot be a valley, and the dictionary is the final arbiter of meaning.[38] No wonder he thinks the Hebrew-Greek distinction "over-dramatized."

How, though, could we go about reading Boman's argument so as to correct its bias? At his most precise, Boman recognizes that when he says "Greek," he is mainly surveying the philosophical writings of Plato. "Hebrew," similarly, stands for a pattern of thought evident in the Hebrew Bible. Thus, he is actually dealing, not with languages, but with texts. "Boman's analysis of the Hebrew mind, however, does not at all touch upon the concept of the text itself and the Jewish relation to it," as Susan Handelman rightly remarks.[39]

In order to raise the question of how "Hebrew thought" enters into the thought processes of an ambivalent Jew like Karl Marx, then, it seems we must open up the typology in three directions. We will take "Hebrew" down into the material world, where it becomes "Jewish." We will travel with "thought" through time and watch it come out "tradition." Finally, "textuality" will emerge from between the lines—those auxiliary lines that Boman forgot to erase—to take on weight and substance and a specifically Jewish coloration. For, as Handelman intimates, it makes all the difference that the text we are scrutinizing is the Torah and that the tradition of reading through which we will seek the meaning of the text is the Jewish tradition. As one Bible scholar observes: "For the Jewish tradition, reading is more than reading: it is a love affair with the text."[40]

III

The Torah is the name Jews apply to the five books of Moses, or Pentateuch, and in a broader sense to the entire set of nearly three dozen books that make up the Hebrew Bible, from Genesis to Chronicles. These writings have been the constant source of Jewish culture. Every week in synagogue for the last two thousand years, observant Jews have heard a portion of the Torah read aloud in Hebrew. The portions fall in a cycle that completes the five books and begins again annually. All other Jewish writings comment on the Torah in one way or another. Indeed, in its broadest sweep, the name "Torah" encompasses all the prophetic writings, legal interpretations, guides to daily conduct, poems, legends, folktales, and mystic doctrines that have ever elaborated on the text, as well as those that have not yet been uttered but will be in the future. The Torah, therefore, is not only text but interpretive process, too—better, it is text understood as process.

For the religious Jew, the Torah summarizes the history of the Jewish tradition: because every generation studies it, the text and its readings to a considerable degree constitute the Jewish experience.[41] According to poet and translator Joel Rosenberg, the books of the Hebrew Bible

> generated a cultural legacy, and the cultural experience they embody and the literary modes they employ are familiar to the Western thinker partly because this reader has learned to read, to some extent, with its eyes.[42]

Because each successive generation learns the Torah all over again, the meanings that its Hebrew words acquire by association with their biblical contexts become part of the social meaning of the words within Hebrew-speaking or Jewish cultures. The literary art that has gone into the composing of the Torah imbues its turns of phrase with a certain way of understanding reality, and study reproduces that understanding in one wave of readers after another.

The text also employs an especially effective device for constructing lasting sets of shared meanings: a system of *leitworter,* or "key-words," plays a large part in the Torah's narrative strategy. Shakespeare critic Bruce Kawin shows how in *King Lear,* key-words bear "the meaning they have acquired with them into their present and future contexts, immensely complicating and interrelating the concerns and actions of the play."[43] So also with the Torah. Just as the imperfect tense of the Hebrew language leaves an action hovering in the air until its effect is no longer felt, so the use of key-words in the Torah also calls the reader to attend to hidden influences and consequences.

When a text uses words in this fashion, they gain an importance over and above their narrow linguistic meaning. To understand what view of reality the Torah truly provides, therefore, we must reunite our care for the ontological implications of the Hebrew language with our attention to biblical content. We must ask what we can learn about a Jewish sense of the world from the plot, characters, and themes of the biblical story.[44]

At first, we might wonder whether we *can* make out any coherent philosophy in such a multivocal body of work as the Torah. Rosenberg, for instance, warns against too "ideological" a reading.

> Given the enormous variety of subjects and literary forms in the Bible, and the long time in which the Hebrew Bible as we now know it coalesced, it is impossible to state *the* message of biblical narrative.[45]

The best summary of biblical narrative, he explains, is the narrative itself. The Torah already uses an extremely compact, highly allusive style, at some points bordering on the cryptic. If we attempt to soak the distinctive hue out of its fabric, we risk dissolving the threads altogether—a risk inherent in any attempt to draw a moral from a piece of literature, but immeasurably sharper in biblical exegesis.

Nevertheless, the same author concludes, with great care, "It *is* possible to speak of 'preoccupations' in biblical narrative, and as such to determine what the narrative is saying." The Torah returns repeatedly to some themes, while yet others seem to influence the story throughout, so much so that without them, the text would be unimaginable. It is entirely legitimate to spell out these central themes, and vitally necessary to do so if we wish to understand how Jewish structures of thought differ from the Western norm, and in what relation Karl Marx stands to each.

The touchstone of reality in the Torah is the active dialogue between God and humankind. By dialogue, we must understand first, actual conversation between two parties. In the storytelling style of the Torah, dialogue predominates. Where the text could have related events in its own voice, it most often makes its characters recount them instead, even if that leaves the narrator only summarizing or confirming assertions already made or just about to be made in speech.

The Torah relies on dialogue rather than description to characterize the actors in its dramas. What individuals say or fail to say,
and when, and how, tells us who they are. Dialogue also suspends
the progress of events and allows for extended scenes of tension
and dramatic irony: one need only look to Abraham's words to
Isaac as they ascend Mount Moriah, or the discourse of Joseph
and his brothers in Egypt, for examples.[46]

In short, "everything in the biblical world ultimately gravitates
toward dialogue," and for good reason. As Robert Alter puts it: "To
the ancient Hebrew writers, speech seemed the essential human
faculty: by exercising the capacity of speech man demonstrated,
however imperfectly, that he was made in the image of God."[47]

Beyond audible speech, however, dialogue means the inescapable relatedness of persons, which is what makes communication between them possible, desirable, and urgent. Martin Buber,
who gave the world the concept of an I-Thou relationship, calls
dialogue "this dramatic over-againstness of God and man, on
which the faith of Israel is grounded."[48] Already in the Talmudic
period, poring over the biblical text, the rabbis had asked the
question: why did God create the world? They answered: because
God was lonely. So the divine Person created human persons, and
so the story which the Bible tells, begins.

The dialogical situation comes about "because God's purposes
are always entrammelled in history, dependent on the acts of individual men and women for their continuing realization." Ever
since the creation, in the Jewish view, it is "human individuality"
which has become "the biblical God's chosen medium for his
experiments with Israel and history."[49]

Within the Torah, human beings are, first and foremost, persons in dialogue with the divine. That communication is what
makes us ourselves, shaping our identities from the core. The
relation of dialogue holds good for all human beings. If the Torah
concentrates on the story of the Jews, that is because, for the
divine experiment the text describes, they form a sort of labora-
tory sample in relationships. If this stiff-necked people can learn
to love and be loved by God, the story intimates, then there is
hope for everyone else, as well.

As a way of engaging the universe, however, dialogue implies an orientation which seems astounding next to any Greek-like model of ontology. The Torah demands of its readers that they seek to know God, not as an eternal set of esoteric truths, but as a distinct personality who speaks and wills, acts and interacts, and to whom they are already committed for life, like a parent or a spouse. The Torah is relatively lacking in theology precisely because what God is lacks interest to the Jewish tradition. Things merely are, perhaps, but God is not a thing. The Torah tries to evoke a sense of what God *wants.* Any aspect of God that does not bear on our personal acquaintance and shared history is pushed to the periphery of its attention. Being human, we think in human terms, even about God. Very well: "The Torah speaks in human language," as one rabbinic saying puts it.[50] It presents God as someone enough like ourselves that consulting our own experience of what people are like will give us a clear enough sense of what the divine Person is like, and how to deal with God.

But then, what is a person in the world of the biblical story? Boman had already remarked: "The person is an active being who is perpetually engaged in becoming and yet remains identical with himself."[51] In dialogical language, we might rephrase it: people become who they are in the process of relating to others, who are also changing and growing, over a period of time.

Now, this does not sound at first like a particularly Jewish idea. Aristotle writes in his *Ethics* of how one's friends crucially affect the development of one's character, for good or ill.[52] In his analysis, however, one person causes changes in another in a predictable, almost mechanical way. Even if the person influenced affects the first person in return, all the effects take place within each individual soul. Moreover, by a certain age, Aristotle believes, the gears of personality have locked into place: one is what one is going to be.

The model of dialogue, on the other hand, presumes that both partners will open themselves to respond and readjust to each other throughout life. Each person will certainly change; it is the relation that will continue. There is also a further difference.

> Cognate with the biblical understanding of individual character as something which develops in and is transformed by time . . . is a sense of character as a center of surprise. This unpredictable and

changing nature of character is one reason why biblical person-
ages cannot have fixed Homeric epithets (Jacob is not "wily Jacob,"
Moses is not "sagacious Moses") but only relational epithets determined by the strategic requirements of the immediate context:
Michal, as the circumstances vary, is either "daughter of Saul" or
"wife of David."[53]

If God, the creator and origin of meaning in the universe, is
conceived in the Torah as a person, and therefore as an essentially relational self who changes as we, God's partners, do—if
God, too, is a "center of surprise"—then relating to God and
participating in the divine purpose must be radically unlike gain-
ing knowledge of the cosmos and contributing to the achievement of a *telos*. Both surely imply a degree of aim and intention.
Both demand movement in a specified direction. Teleological development, however, aims at a fixed goal that human beings can
only discover, not shape, while partnership with God allows for
discussion, revision, disagreement, and reconciliation.

Teleology hinges on epistemology. One can only succeed at
reaching one's highest state if one can correctly ascertain that in
which it consists and those intermediate steps one must take to
arrive there. For the dialogical relation, on the other hand, the
best parallel is probably a good marriage. The lovers, over time,
learn each other intimately, even if they only learn some important facts about each other after many years, or never. They
know the important things—what makes the loved one happy,
depressed, nervous, serene, comfortable, irritated, frightened,
secure—in a rudimentary way from near the beginning. What
they discover is the range of one another's reactions, not the rules
of them. Day by day, they take note of the changes in each other's
lives and work to adapt to them together. At times, unavoidably,
one or the other will become withdrawn or fall out of sync; at
such times, their commitment to what they share carries them
through. On the basis of trust, without needing or seeking perfect knowledge, they create a small world that shelters them both.

The dialogue which the Torah records between God and the
Jewish people, and potentially between God and all humanity,
aspires to exactly this kind of marriage for the renewal of the
larger world. As Buber puts it:

The real communion of man with God not only has its place in the world, but also its subject. God speaks to man in the things and beings that He sends him in life; man answers in relation to just these things and beings.[54]

One final lesson that the Torah teaches us about a Jewish sense of reality, we must not overlook. In the biblical story, human action is undertaken freely even though God has purposes which only human beings can work out. "Put most simply," says Rosenberg, "persons are free to act as they will, but their actions are fateful."[55] By creating the world in a fit of loneliness, the God of the Torah has voluntarily become dependent on the notoriously perverse and inconsistent powers of human will and action.

As compared to Greek myth (in which mortals and gods alike await the designs of Fate), Greek philosophy (in which the universe allows for human excellence but neither promotes nor needs it), and those elements of Christianity that stress predestination, original sin, and undeserved divine grace, the Jewish themes of dialogue and partnership in creation mean that people and their actions *matter*. That sense of the cosmic importance of human action is a thread that leads us straight into the Marxian labyrinth.

CHAPTER 3

Greek
and Hebrew
in Marx's
Ontology

WHEN WE EXAMINE the body of Marx's writings, in works as dissimilar as Marx's doctoral dissertation and *The German Ideology*, we find hints that Marx himself recognizes a Jewish-Greek distinction among ways of characterizing reality.

We do not have to look far to discover the importance Marx attaches to Greek thought and culture. For nearly ten years, from 1837 to 1846, classical Greece figures prominently in Marx's writing. Unlike his contemporaries, however, Marx treats the glory that was Greece as a cautionary tale. He dissents from "the admiration, even worship for classical Greece" which had buoyed German literature in the late eighteenth century, and which still showed its influence on Hegel.[1]

Marx instead regards the Greek city-state, the *polis*, as an attempt at freedom that failed. The lesson he draws from its collapse is that trying to reunite the worlds of thought and action by means of philosophy alone is futile. Philosophy inevitably raises up some partial, one-sided view of reality to the level of Truth, suppressing other equally compelling perspectives. Thus, in Marx's vocabulary Greece stands for a typically "Greek" bias in thinking, according to the model of Greek thought we have discussed. By the same token, when Marx criticizes the Greek approach, his critique seems to arise from something distinctly resembling a Jewish standpoint on what can plausibly be called real.

I

For many of the German Romantic thinkers of the late 1700s, according to Charles Taylor, the ancient Greeks presented an inspiring portrait of

> a mode of life in which the highest in man, his aspiration to form and expression and clarity was at one with his nature and all of nature. It was an era of unity and harmony within man, in which thought and feeling, morality and sensibility were one, in which the form which man stamped on his life whether moral, political or spiritual flowed from his own natural being, and was not imposed on it by the force of raw will.[2]

Hegel, the "gigantic thinker" of Marx's young adulthood, offered a more nuanced but scarcely less laudatory version.[3] Like the Romantics, he saw the *polis* as both a realization of the human essence and its most adequate expression to date. At its height, he theorized, classical Greece harmonized being and thought, the individual and the community. Citizens knew their place in the natural and the political order and acted in keeping with that knowledge. Human beings related to the *polis* in which they lived, and its ideals, as particulars to a universal. They lived as instances of the state; its existence embodied itself in theirs. They enjoyed freedom, not in unrestraint, but in the achievement of the virtues praised by the ethos of their community. Political life, in Hegel's picture of Greek culture, supplied the definition of those virtues, and hence politics was the precondition of human freedom.

The happy unity Hegel envisioned did contain a fatal flaw, however: its parochiality. Hegel argued that the integrity of any Greek city-state was not really universal but only, in Taylor's words, "the spirit of a people, one among many."[4] Its cohesiveness was achieved by sacrificing reflection. Most citizens of the *polis* knew only one way of life, their own.

In time, some deeply spiritual individuals (notably Socrates) would rebel, seeking a larger unity and a consciousness too broad

for any particular *polis*. Because they were only individuals, however, they could not embody universal truths. Simply by being
finite and particular themselves, Hegel contends, they would be
inadequate to the task. So, Hegel concludes, people like Socrates
had to challenge the societies in which they lived to transcend the
limited notions of the good human life their citizens uncritically
accepted. In doing so, however, these universal thinkers began
a tragic struggle which sometimes destroyed them and always
fractured the unified, if one-sided, cultures that had given them
birth.

Hegel celebrates the achievements of the *polis* and mourns its
passing, but he thinks its demise necessary for the recapture of
human freedom at a higher level. His philosophy represents a
commitment to the idea of a society in which neither Socrates nor
Jesus would have had to die in order to be heard.[5] All nations,
classes, and philosophies would find a home within the complex
structure of such a society. The state he hoped for would express,
and therefore reconcile, the totality of its citizens' beings, while
their lives would give substance to the ideal of an expressive unity
in nature.

Marx takes over Hegel's idea of a connection between the ancient Greek republic and the ideal of unity when he "goes over to"
Hegelianism in 1837, but with a dramatic difference. From the
outset, Marx treats classical Greece as a failure in the pursuit of
that ideal, and not as a historically limited form of its realization.

Marx's distinct viewpoint emerges most clearly when he ana-
lyzes the position of the philosopher in Greek culture. Hegel had
considered the classic thinkers of Greece as shoots of a living
culture from which they drew their intellectual and spiritual
sustenance. Their thinking, he believed, reflected their civic life.
Marx draws the opposite conclusion. "The Greek philosopher is a
demiurge," he writes in a preparatory note for his dissertation.
"His world is other than the one that flourishes in the natural sun
of substantial existence."[6]

The very idea of wisdom in Greece, according to Marx, arose
from individual thinkers' reflections on their private experience,
in abstraction from the life of their community. Far from display-
ing the unity of the ideal and the real in Greek communal life,

these *sophoi*, these "wise ones" negated it by walling themselves off in a world of their own imagining and calling it "spiritual truth." In the way that they lived their own lives, the philosophers estranged thinking from living. They also created a realm of pure thought called "philosophy" and fenced it off from the public domain.

If the Greeks ever experienced the wholeness Hegel envisioned for them, Marx dates it far earlier than the classical age, possibly even before philosophy was invented at all. By the time of Socrates, certainly, the "split between reason and existence reached full expression" in Greek communal life. Socrates, writes Marx, is not a victim of a society he challenges. Rather, Socrates embodies the inner conflicts of the *polis* and succumbs to them. "Divided within himself" so deeply that his own ethical impulses seemed to him a *daimon* or indwelling spirit, "condemned" to generate chimerical visions of a good life that his own nation could not make real, in Marx's judgment, Socrates went to his death in vain. His fate reveals "the relationship of Greek philosophy to Greek life and thereby its inner contraction into itself."[7]

In the main body of his dissertation, Marx frames his critiques of Greek thought in a different way: by showing how the opposition of thought and life played itself out in the lives of two lesser Greek philosophers, Epicurus and Democritus. Each of them represents to Marx one horn of the Greek dilemma, and each lands himself in a web of insoluble contradictions.

Epicurus, as Marx portrays him, is a dogmatic idealist. In his theory of nature, atoms (which are literally the basic units of reality) must tend to swerve from the paths that the forces of gravity and mutual repulsion mark out for them. They must swerve simply in order to show that being does not wholly submit to material laws. Now, the unpredictability Epicurus's view entails should have thrust him out into the physical world to search for contingent truths. If he had done so, however, he would be conceding that the ability of any individual consciousness to get at the truth depends on material forces external to the individual. This would have contradicted the basic principle which (on Marx's reading) led him to hypothesize the atomic swerve in the first place. Consequently, Marx argues, Epicurus actually neglected empirical studies and led a static, sedentary, and untroubled life.[8]

Democritus, on the other hand, is a staunch materialist. He founds his atomic theory on the assumption that atoms are law-abiding particles: their set motions explain all that exists. As Marx reads him, however, Democritus, too, confronts a paradox. He believes that no natural phenomenon makes the presence of atoms observable to the human eye. The materially based regularities never disclose themselves, while the apparent world, which the senses cannot deny, is all chaos and deception.

> Democritus, for whom the principal element does not enter appearance and remains without reality and existence, is on the other hand faced with the world of sensible perception as a real and concrete world. This world is, to be sure, subjective illusion, but just because of this, it is torn free from the principal element, left in its autonomous reality; at the same time it is the unique, the real object, and as such has value and importance.[9]

Consequently, Democritus roamed the known world, accumulating endless data about the "subjective illusion" which is all the reality he is granted. Legend has it that he ended his fruitless quest for positive knowledge by blinding himself, "so that the sensible light in the eye would not darken sharpness of intellect."[10]

According to Marx's prognosis, Epicurus, Democritus, and Socrates all fail because of the same cultural bent in Greek philosophy: the belief that thought can comprehend itself in isolation from life. More concretely, the Greeks believe that a thinker can discover the truth about human nature outside of his or her social relations with other human beings. This feature of Greek philosophy is also one of the major differences between Greek and Jewish thought, so it is significant that Marx uses it to criticize the Greeks.

II

Marx accuses modern philosophers of repeating the errors of the ancients. Once again, he charges, they pretend to be able to devise a better world without engaging the one they presently inhabit. Modern philosophy, it seems to Marx, has inherited the

Greek disposition to exalt the stance of the spectator and to choose contemplation, rather than interaction, as the preferred way of learning about reality. This, too, ranges Marx against the Hellenic influence from a standpoint which resembles the Jewish one. Since he groups moderns with Greeks, Marx passes harsh judgment on nearly all political thought.

The one great exception is Hegel. For the youthful Marx, Hegel had promised a way "to seek the ideal in the real itself,"[11] and thereby to avoid the "inner contraction into itself" which he thought had doomed Greek philosophy. From 1837 until 1841, in fact, Marx prescribed Hegel's holistic approach as the antidote to metaphysical systems which write the philosopher's consciousness large and call that reality. By 1843, of course, Marx changed his mind about the usefulness of Hegel. In the *Critique of Hegel's "Philosophy of Right,"* written two years after his dissertation and shortly before "On the Jewish Question," Marx accuses his former mentor of reducing the individual to "his beard and blood" and abstracting from social contexts and relations.[12]

Marx's putative break with Hegel has been much explored, but one thing that has not been widely discussed is how, in order to settle accounts with Hegel, Marx begins more and more to read him as a Greek. In the *Critique* just mentioned, Marx likens Hegel to Socrates. Neither, he declares, is "allowed to measure the idea by what exists; he must measure what exists by the idea." In the *1844 Manuscripts,* he expands on this comparison. Both Socrates and Hegel display "the opposition, within thought itself, between abstract thinking and sensuous reality or real sensuousness." In addition, Hegel begins to resemble Epicurus. As Jerrold Seigel points out:

> With Hegel, "abstraction resolves to forsake abstraction and to have a look at nature free from abstraction." But just as Epicurus in the end merely gave objective form to his abstract thinking, so for Hegel, too . . . nature already existed in the thinker's mind as an image of his own activity, and "what he has really let emerge from himself is only this *abstract nature,* only nature as a thought-entity—but now with the significance that it is the other-being of thought."[13]

Where Marx had earlier honored Hegel as the philosopher of "the whole," he increasingly rereads him as just another partial thinker. Like the ancients, Hegel takes his own end (defined by

Marx as "constructing the hereditary monarch out of the pure Idea")[14] for the end of society.

Later, when Marx shifts his theoretical stance even further in *The German Ideology*, he continues to set himself apart from his former associates by pointing out the specific defects they share with the Greeks. For instance, he and Engels deride the German "true socialists" by claiming they convert the practical program of the French socialist party into a set of timeless truths. Thinkers of Marx's day, Marx asserts, follow the Greeks in inverting the relation of being and thought, and they cannot help doing so once they eternalize their own perspective in a characteristically Greek way.[15]

In short, something very much like the critique of Greek thought from a Jewish point of view shows up in the center of Marx's critique of German philosophy. Typically, he does not endorse Jewish thought and decry Greek thought so much as pronounce a judgment on the effects of adopting either. Marx clearly regards "Greek" attempts to establish the real on a higher plane than the everyday as a mistake, a chimera, even a self-delusion. Yet even if this speculative vision of reality conformed to the facts, it would provide no basis for the harmonious social order its proponents seek to achieve. To say that all people and all activities contribute to an expressive unity of human existence but that only people who are philosophers (or ordinary people while thinking philosophically) can experience it as such, is to say that no such unity exists, by any standard Marx would accept.

As long as a society systematically excludes certain categories of people, activities, experiences, or states of mind from its normative version of what is real, it is still parochial, abstract, and less than fully human. Therefore, Marx demands that any acceptable ontology provide for the possibility that humanity can achieve a genuine social whole, which he calls "species-being" or "human emancipation," and later, "communism." Any other definition of the human is self-defeating. Therefore, also, Marx is drawn to the sense of the real he associates with civil society and with the Jewish outlook. In its emphasis on human action directed toward the effective overcoming of practical human need, what he terms the "Jewish" outlook offers Marx a more trustworthy guide than philosophy to what must be done. Starting from it, he believes he can realize the wholeness of which philosophers may only dream.[16]

III

The way of understanding reality that Marx calls Jewish fits the pattern of Jewish thought much as his image of Greek culture fits Greek thought as a type. Turning to the Jewish side, however, we cannot make the connection unless we make a distinction once again between "sabbath" and "everyday" Judaism. Marx, as we noted earlier, holds no brief for the Jewish religion, nor does he think it important as a religion. This judgment does not necessarily stem from ignorance, either. Marx displays a certain ease with biblical texts. Often, when he needs a good pungent example in order to make a point, he reaches for the name of a biblical character: Moses, Joshua, the Levites, Adam, Esau, Habakkuk, and Ezekiel all pop up in his writings.[17]

These references demonstrate Marx's familiarity with the Bible as literature—probably attained in the *Gymnasium* under a Lutheran teacher. Clearly, though, they have no bearing on his ontology. Any educated German of Marx's day would have read the Bible along with works of Shakespeare and Goethe, these being regarded as the cornerstones of German culture.

Nor is there anything especially Jewish about Marx's handling of his biblical allusions. It is of interest that Marx rarely, if ever, resorts to the Gospels or any part of the Christian canon for an illustration. His Bible is strictly "Old Testament."[18] Still, one cannot make much of that. Paradoxically, then, at those moments when he touches on the content of Jewish faith, Marx tells us virtually nothing about his relation or nonrelation to Jewish thought.

But perhaps we are looking for Jewish thought the wrong way. Perhaps Jewish thought exerts itself in Marx's theory the way that atoms do in Democritus's physics: as a "principal element [which] does not enter appearance" but which nonetheless unifies all the rest. "Even with philosophers who give their work a systematic form," Marx writes, ". . . the true inner structure is different from the form in which the philosopher consciously presents it."[19] For Marx, we remember, the key to Epicurean philosophy was the atomic swerve, which revealed that philosopher's notion of freedom. The "inner structure" of Marx's work which shows its affinity for Jewish thought is his ontology. Bertell Ollman has outlined its main points.

First, Marx views the world as a system of internal relations. Nothing exists on its own, discretely, independent of all else, nor do things simply happen to come into association by external contingency or chance. Anything which is, is by virtue of its interrelation with other features of reality. In Marx's theory, things only take on a definite existence through interaction. To be exact, Ollman suggests, we should call this play in the fabric of the universe "*inner*action," since all the reciprocal effects which finally characterize any object occur within the totality of things real, and not between independently real units.[20]

For Marx, however odd it may seem for a famous materialist, things as such do not exist. All the factors he examines (labor, capital, land), he first has to distinguish from the whole. Furthermore, for different purposes, he individuates them in different ways. In Marx's ontology, a thing will not be defined by listing its qualities. Instead, Marx will vary the attributes he counts as pertinent to an object of his scrutiny depending on the specific set of relations in which he is locating it at the moment. Capital, for example, can just as easily mean "control of the means of production" or "control of the means of exploiting and subjecting the laborer." In Marx's full theoretical conception, of course, it means both. As Ollman explains:

> Essentially, a change of focus has occurred from viewing independent factors which are related, to viewing the particular way in which they are related in each factor, to grasping this tie as part of the meaning conveyed by the concept. This view does not rule out the existence of a core notion for each factor, but treats this core notion itself as a cluster of relations.[21]

When Marx actively determines which relations he will take to constitute a thing under discussion, he is only doing what he believes human beings do all the time: namely, appropriating the world. The term "appropriation" points to the special place Marx's ontology accords to human beings. Like all the animals, species *homo sapiens* intrinsically belongs to the natural world. "A being which does not have its true nature outside of itself," Marx proclaims, "is not a *natural* being and does not share in the being of nature."[22] Nature is "Man's inorganic body." Yet human beings are not sunk into their physical environment, either. Both in thought and action, we grapple with nature in ways that materially change it, and ourselves as part of it. Other animals coexist with their surroundings. Human beings struggle in order to make the world our own in some way, and to leave our mark upon it. The process of appropriation marks off those relations by which, from then on, we will recognize the factors that we incorporate into our own existence.

For Marx, the most characteristically human way of orienting the world, and thus of shaping it, is through labor. Merely looking at a beautiful sunset, for example, we change ourselves by heightening our sensitivity to beauty. We appropriate it: it becomes a part of us. If we go on to paint the sunset, however, or to picture it in words, we capture it in a richer, deeper way. By making the objects of our sense perceptions into the objects of our expression, we bring a wider range of our human capacities to bear on them. We establish a more all-around, fully human relation to the sunset, and in the process, we become more human ourselves. Marx views things as the summary of relations, and therefore he can equally well call human interaction with nature "the appropriation of the human essence."[23] Human beings only *are* in relation to the world; we can only reveal what we may be by acting on objects.

What is this "human essence" of which Marx speaks? Marx denies that any fixed set of descriptions can apply to humanity in all ages and countries. Such stereotyping is one of the items he dismisses under the label "ideology." He does assert, however, that human beings as a species possess a definite set of shared needs. Human needs impel us to appropriate the world. "The need of a thing," Marx writes, "is the evident, irrefutable proof that the thing belongs to my being."[24]

The needs we feel stem from the powers we possess. Human powers range from the five senses to procreation, will, judgment, sex, love, and other varied capacities.[25] Marx declares that even the most basic faculties, such as smelling and tasting, can be employed in either an animal or a human fashion. Progress consists in part of satisfying needs in a more human manner, and in part of cultivating new needs that extend our range and bring us more fully into relation with the world.

While individuals must make an effort if they wish to realize their intrinsic powers, the progress in which Marx takes his keenest interest depends on changes at a social level. The mode in which a society produces, trying to satisfy human needs, is not a matter of individual choice. The mode of production, rather, sets human beings into definite social relations; these in turn will go a long way toward generating one's current needs. Paradoxically, how human beings conceive of their own powers will depend mainly on how the mode of production by which they live, which they themselves erect and maintain, teaches them to understand what they need. Under capitalism especially, a social formation that people have created reacts cruelly back upon them to limit their further social creativity. [26]

Carol Gould has called Marx's theory a *social ontology,* an "analysis of the nature of social reality by means of socially interpreted categories." [27] Most people, however, do not operate with such an analysis. Instead, they take their cues as to what they need and what they can achieve from what they observe to be possible under existing social arrangements. They are thus brought to deny the impulse to develop their human powers, those very same powers that brought them to their present pass.

> Private property has made us so stupid and partial that an object is only *ours* when we have it, when it exists for us as capital, or when it is directly eaten, drunk, worn, inhabited, etc., in short, *utilized* in some way. [28]

As Marx argues, however, when we opt for our present practical needs, people (for instance, the Jews in "On the Jewish Question") are not simply deceived. The mode of production by which we survive *actually* contradicts the need to become what one needs to be. Popular consciousness accurately reflects an impossible reality. People experience the world as alien and overpowering because it has really become alienated from them and dominant over them.

Because Marx's ontology takes relational human beings, social processes, and changing human needs as its basic matter, it is simultaneously an ontology and a philosophy of history. Human history, in Marx's telling, shares many features with a well-told story. Its hero is the human species; its villain, disintegrated existence. Its plot revolves around the conflict between human needs and the unsuccessful attempts to fulfill them which have tragically become necessary to survival.

If, in the famous slogan which opens the *Communist Manifesto*, all history is indeed "the history of class struggle," that is because each class, in accordance with its place in the mode of production, seizes on certain powers, needs, and ways of appropriating the world. Each class fights to reorganize society so as to emancipate its particular human capacities.[29] The purveyors of these partial solutions, even when they revolutionize society, typically fail to realize the full significance of their actions. For Marx, however, one can only "realize" meaning—that is, make it real—through action. He takes practice and not consciousness as the true expression of what the species has become.

The most human way to create social structures, nonetheless, is in full awareness of the needs we seek to meet, and the ways certain practices succeed better than others at that task, and (to the extent to which we can anticipate it) the transforming of human powers that will result from such practices. Marx sees the alienation of labor as a force which both prevents this kind of awareness and demands it. Theory, on the other hand, aids its rise. Theorizing, then, is a part of making history, and thinking, acting human beings are the center of the historical narrative. To break out of the trap set by alienated labor and to return to the free-yet-directed pursuit of species-being: that is the purpose that relates one moment of history to the next.

IV

Over and over again in this account, we find that Marx's sense of what is real escapes the confines of the Greek conception of "being." Ultimate reality to the Greeks is spiritual; to Marx, it must be rooted in the material. Each real thing in Greek thought has a single essence; in Marx's view, all things are constituted in relation to one another. Observing and contemplating the world are the highest human activities Greek thought can imagine, and theory is their expression. For Marx, on the other hand, human beings at their best strive to appropriate and transform the world, through productive practice. Consequently, Marx thinks of the realization of the world as an inherently social endeavor, unlike the Greek pursuit of truth, which is a matter for individual philosophers. Also, Marx finds meaning in historical change, in contrast to the Greek view that only the eternal and the immutable truly signify.

Finally, because of the dialectical quality of human needs (that one set of needs, being fulfilled, produces a richer set), Marx cannot project a Republic, an Absolute State, or any vision of the world made whole once and for all. Human history is not approaching an ideal form, or a *telos*, or any goal given in advance and always potentially present. Instead, as Marx understands it, we are tacking toward a goal which changes as we near it—and so do we.[30] Within the constraints of material conditions which our past actions have helped to shape, impelled by needs that we ourselves have in part produced, we continually redefine the good human life we are seeking. That conception of human activity sets Marx apart, both from ancient thinkers who give life a predetermined end, and from moderns who make all ends a matter of arbitrary and individual choice.

It sets him apart, however, only if we allow it to do so. Many, probably most, of Marx's commentators look at his ontology and do not recognize the dialogical pattern we have traced there. Both those who speak on Marx's behalf and those who argue against him agree that he thinks teleologically—that he is working toward an end which itself propels history to a predetermined conclusion. Ollman, for instance, assigns communism a foundational role for Marx's philosophy. Not only does he measure everything by the standard of "after the revolution," but also he insists that we must interpret every part of Marx's ontology in terms of its contribution toward producing "communist Man" and his powers.[31] So limitless are the capacities he ascribes to this new breed, too, that he opens Marx to the charge of making people into abstractions all over again.[32]

This is surely no service to Marx. For it is precisely in reaction to this kind of "Marxism" that Taylor, for one, claims Marx's concept of freedom must ultimately be incoherent. Marx's theory, according to Taylor, can only find any purpose for human strivings as long as the end of the theory—creating the conditions for human freedom—are still not met. "But once the conditions are realized, the Marxist notion of freedom is of no further help." Why is this? "The overcoming of all alienation and division leaves man without a situation"; that is, without any "predicament which sets us a certain task or calls for a certain response from us if we are to be free." Marx's theoretical end unravels itself, and so, Taylor contends, Marx's is a notion of "an utterly empty freedom."[33]

We can appreciate the force of this argument. In effect, it claims that Marx, despite all his efforts, has produced still too Greek a solution. At the end, it still fails to emancipate the real, individual human beings. Marx could not shrug off this thrust; it strikes at the heart of his concern, the reason for his theorizing.

Moreover, Marx himself provides support for the indictment in the later pages of *Capital*, where he speaks of expanding the realm of freedom and contracting the realm of necessity.[34] This approach clashes harshly with his main argument that needs spur the humanizing of *all* human activity. The idea that we can, and should, minimize the portion of our lives devoted to need suggests that freedom consists of acting without reference to the specific powers whose exercise we care about, and which have historically defined what it means to be human. This freedom certainly resembles Taylor's "situationless freedom." It even smells of Nietzsche's "passive nihilism."[35]

Like Ollman's exaggerated defense, however, Taylor's critique takes it for granted that the teleological reading of Marx is the only one we can accept. What if we choose not to do so? We have before us an alternative: the dialogical reading. As it appears in Jewish thought, dialogue has a direction: it leads somewhere we want and need to go. But its goal, hallowing the world, is itself a process which calls for ever freer and more purposeful dialogue.

In the dialogical relation, that is to say, we can make progress and perceive that we are making progress without measuring it off against a fixed goal or *telos*. Similarly, Marx's theory of emancipation does not have to depend on a final smoothing out of contradictions for us to feel its liberatory thrust. We can accept it as an interpretation without requiring any other "proof" than its ability to capture for us our felt needs and the tasks they impose—what Marx might call our "situation in the present enslaved world."[36]

We might therefore read Marx's theory as a story with a plot and a climax but no ending, only, in Taylor's terms, "a bent in things which inclines without necessitating."[37] This sort of reading would relieve us of the paradox of a freedom which dissolves once it is fully achieved. A non-"Marxist" appropriation of Marx's ontology makes room for the actual experience of historically concrete human beings; it allows that experience to influence their decisions about how they will go about coming free and what to do with that freedom once they enjoy it. Since one of Marx's criticisms of Greek and modern theorists is that they shut out real people, admitting them only as "the other-being of thought,"[38] a reading of Marx which lets them back in can plausibly claim to keep faith with Marx's project.

The interpretation we have developed here also gains credence from its affinity with the theme of *partnership with God* we encountered in Jewish thought. God nowhere appears as a real actor in Marx's theory. Nevertheless, in Marx as in the Torah, human beings take part in the continuous creation of the world. Human action bears a cosmic significance. People are engaged in a historic mission, and we sense a direction to our actions which seems to respond both to our wills and to something real and effective beyond ourselves. With all these points of contact, it would not be surprising if Marx's sense of reality embraced one more Jewish theme: a goal which we help shape, even as we struggle to make it real.

V

Is Marx's ontology Jewish? It is, and yet it is not. Despite his remarks about "the negation of Judaism" as a starting point, Marx does not select the Jews as his chosen people. The history he finds meaningful is economic, political, cultural, but not religious and not the Torah. God disappears from Marx. What stands in dialogue with human need is a complex of "Nature" and "Man," or the physical environment and the way human beings have worked and are continuing to work on it. Nature and past human activities compose the human situation. They set the conditions and provide the impulse and the raw materials for fulfilling human needs. All needs are human, though. There are no others.

Marx thus sets himself the puzzle of meeting the demands a Jewish sense of reality places upon him while rejecting the traditional source of answers for how to do so. His is a dialogue with an exiled God. The rabbis of the Talmudic period faced a similar crisis of interpretation, and they resolved it by subjecting the Torah to a series of daring reinterpretations.[39] Marx's solution is even more difficult: he must do his exegesis on the "text" of the social fabric itself.

Nevertheless, as a first reading Marx can and does engage the special part of social practice which tries to encapsulate the rest: the writing of theory. As a reader of Hegel, in particular, Marx brings into profane political theory a style of hermeneutics which is and is not the same as the rabbinic mode of interpretation called *midrash*. Not only do his purposes spring from a refracted version of Jewish reality, but his methods do, as well.

CHAPTER 4

Reading and Writing Marx

> What do you do when the text you are studying doesn't make
> sense? The sense it would make is inseparable from the reason
> you are studying it in the first place (what is it that you wish to
> know?). This question may be asked in a different way: What
> would this text have to become in order for you to make sense of
> it? Or again: What sense are you inclined to make of it?—
> Gerald L. Bruns, *Inventions*

AT THIS POINT, I hope, some readers are following
the story of the Jewish question about Marx with excitement: as
if, through a window, they had glimpsed a childhood friend passing by and rushed out to greet him. Others, no doubt, are scan-
ning these lines with growing impatience. Unwilling to suspend
disbelief so long, they are wondering why we have passed over
what seems to them an obvious question: namely, what about
Hegel? Instead of postulating a complex and conflicted relation
between Marx's theory and Jewish structures of thought, could
we not trace the ways Marx diverges from Greek ontology to the
influence of Hegel's dialectic? That is the way the story is usually
told, and it has the comfort of placing Marx in the context of a
thinker he actually studied. It may be true as we have argued that
Marx ultimately rejected Hegel for being too "Greek," but Marx
rejected Judaism, too. If we choose to read Marx through the lens
of Jewish thought, then what shall we say about Hegel?

The idea that in order to produce his own theory Marx simply
inverts the Hegelian system originates with Marx himself. "My
dialectic method," he asserts in an afterword to the second German edition of *Capital*, "is not only different from the Hegelian,
but is its direct opposite."

> To Hegel, the life-process of the human brain, i.e., the process of thinking, which, under the name of "the Idea," he even transforms into an independent subject, is the demiurgos [creator] of the real world, and the real world is only the external, phenomenal form of "the Idea." With me, on the contrary, the ideal is nothing else than the material world reflected by the human mind, and translated into forms of thought. . . .
>
>   . . . With him [the dialectic] is standing on its head. It must be turned right side up again, if you would discover the rational kernel within the mystical shell. [1]

Twentieth-century writers who treat of Marx's debt to Hegel take Marx literally. They accept on faith that he inverted the idealist dialectic while preserving its basic motions. For instance, Avineri states:

> From a systematic point of view the difference between Marx and Hegel in this respect can be reduced to Marx's rejection of the Hegelian postulate about the existence of a super-historical essence, Absolute Spirit, and to his contention that the *Aufhebung* [transcendence] of the antagonism has yet to occur, while Hegel thought it had already occurred. [2]

These differences, however "reduced," do put Marx at odds with Hegel. Whether the world is already redeemed (with Jesus) or whether it still awaits its redemption in history is a fundamental question. Indeed, it is the issue that most obviously divides Judaism from Christianity, and has for two thousand years. [3] Still, on the widely accepted view, all that separates Marx from Hegel is a simple opposition. They disagree only on the facts, while they share an understanding of reality in which, sometime, all contradictions will be resolved.

And in fact, it is possible for the sympathetic reader to assimilate much of Marx's ontology to Hegel's dialectic. Like Marx and unlike many thinkers of his time, Hegel understands the world as constituted by tensions between opposing forces, or "contradictions." He looks for these contradictions to produce new configurations of events and of ideas. Hegel's philosophy is *dynamic*—it studies reality in flux—and *progressive*—it both "gains in richness" as it examines each era of history in turn and "moves toward the realization of a final good." [4] It is therefore intrinsically temporal and historical, unlike Greek thought and like Marx's. For all these reasons, commentators have agreed that

Marx's theory begins as a materialist critique of Hegel's idealist logic. Wherever Hegel writes *Spirit*, Marx simply substitutes *Man*, and proceeds from there.[5]

Since so much of Marx's thinking about the nature of reality can plausibly be read as Hegel turned right-side up, and since that reading carries with it the weight of a long and venerable tradition, what gives us the effrontery to suggest an alternative? Primarily, it is the nagging sense that the accepted formula is just too neat. The transposition it demands sounds too smooth to describe the way any thinker draws on another, let alone a thinker who holds Marx's philosophy of writing.

As we recall, Marx regards already existing texts, his own included, as opportunities. Nothing is written in stone: everything sooner or later requires revision. "An author . . . cannot publish *literally* what he has written six months previously."[6] If Marx read Hegel's *Philosophy of Right*, written a great deal more than six months prior, the way he read his own writing, he would seek out gaps, contradictions, and questions left dangling in the air that gave him room to push his own investigations further. This continual probing hardly jibes with the image Marx offers us of "standing Hegel right-side up again" once and for all.

We may wonder at Marx's story of his appropriation of Hegel, since compared to his philosophy of writing it strikes a hollow note. We have two other reasons to suspect Marx's account of his relation to Hegel. The formula of Hegel upside-down does not reflect all of what Marx says about how he reads Hegel. It also misleads us about what happens as the result of his reading. Let us examine these objections more closely.

When Marx himself explains his compulsion to transcend his teacher, in the 1843 *Contribution to the Critique of Hegel's "Philosophy of Right,"* he does criticize the latter's "spiritual" bent. As we saw in chapter 3, however, he also condemns Hegel's ontology because it is "Greek": it excludes certain basic aspects of human life, and therefore certain persons in society, from full participation in human freedom. The vision of the whole which Marx justly or unjustly imputes to Hegel makes truth (and consequently, freedom) accessible only from a philosophical standpoint, either to philosophers themselves or to those who adopt a similar God's-eye view of the universe. For Marx, this is a deformed understanding of human emancipation.

Reading Marx, then, we observe him attacking Hegel on two fronts at once: on his casting Spirit, and not humanity, as the hero of his story, and on his willingness to exclude major elements of human life from his ideal of human freedom. At best, a reversal of Hegel would only answer the first of the two charges, leaving the second unopposed. Furthermore, these are not trivial points. They strike at the heart of Hegel's theory as Marx interprets it. Is it at all likely that Marx had never thought of them before he read Hegel, and that the main points of his own theory occurred to him only as the "direct opposite" of the *Philosophy of Right?* What can Marx mean by "turning Hegel right-side up again"?

In order to arrive at an answer, we must listen to what the memorable phrase about Hegel is saying. To speak of the dialectic standing on its head is to employ a trope of inversion, reversal, or exchange of place. Like an hourglass in which all the sand has fallen to the bottom, the dialectic as it is found with Hegel can be righted, so that what had settled can be set into motion again. Once right-side up, however, neither the structure nor the content will change. The two sides of an hourglass are identical. So, if we were to read "standing on its head" as a simple metaphor, we would expect God to take the place of Man and Man of God in Marx's theory and all the relations between them to remain the same, although flowing toward the opposite pole from before.

This is not what happens when Marx reads Hegel. Indeed, it is hard to imagine how it could be. In Hegel's dialectic, human beings in their finitude and morality embody a necessary moment in the process by which Spirit becomes real in the world. Although that process reaches on beyond them, human beings are among its atoms, its constituent elements: they could not be left out.

For Marx, matters stand quite differently. Unlike humanity to the dialectic of Spirit, God is not essential to the development of the human species. Rather, God (or the belief in God) is an obstruction to that development, according to Marx. Human emancipation does not incorporate religion but abolishes it, instead. It does the same to the state, thus dispensing with an institution Hegel regards as crucial to the realization of Absolute Spirit. Even culture and consciousness, the other denizens of Hegel's "realm of the spirit," take on a shadowy half-life in those parts of Marx's writings which are a critique of Hegel. It is as if Marx were so offended by Hegel's subordination of humanity to "the Idea" that he could not stand to focus on anything else in Hegel for long.

I

If we want to understand why Marx has to remove Spirit from the dialectic and not just reverse its place within it, we may consider a crucial presupposition of the Hegelian philosophy which Taylor describes.

> The universe has many levels because it is the unfolding of an inner necessity in external reality. The infinite end is realized in finite ends. *And that is why we can see the end of Reason both as always realized and as always having to be realized.* The experience of finite subjects is that the plan of reason has yet to be fulfilled. They strive towards it. But if we rise to a vision of the whole we can see that this very striving is part of the plan and that as a whole it is already realized. The appearance of unrealizedness is an error, a deception; and yet this deception itself is brought about by the Idea, as is the overcoming of this error by ourselves.[7]

This is a comforting conclusion. In order to arrive at it, though, Hegel has to make two further assumptions. First, there is a "vision of the whole," a privileged perspective from which "external" reality all makes sense. Second, we can know that this perspective is the true one, and that the more mundane perspective which sees the world as still fragmented and incomplete is "an error, a deception." In positing a point of view which is both true and certain, Hegel aspires to what we called a moment ago a "God's-eye view of the universe."

When Marx removes God from the dialectic, however, he at the same time rejects the God's-eye viewpoint or anything like it. "The experience of finite subjects" is all we have to go on. Denying our finitude would lead us to spin cobweb worlds out of our own heads, as Marx accuses the Greek philosophers of doing. On the other hand, denying that we are subjects in the plural (and not some singular world-spirit) would open the door again for some class of people falsely to proclaim itself the universal, ignoring the experience and the needs of others.[8] So, from the beginning, the theoretical move that excludes God from the dialectic has a political bearing. If God did not exist, Marx would still be forced to deny Him—in order to refute the godlike pretensions of certain human beings.

By now, we begin to detect a pattern into which Marx's swerve away from Hegel fits. It is just the same turn Marx makes from Bauer in "On the Jewish Question" by denying that political emancipation from religion, property, and so on can be a real liberation. Marx is also exhibiting the same penchant when he rejects the claims of the political state, "the perfected Christian state," to unify and free society, and again when he leaves the *polis* and Greek philosophy behind as models for fulfilled human life and thought. In *Capital*, Marx returns to expand on the same progression. First, he reconstructs the commonplace notion of free exchange in the marketplace. He reveals by its absence what that notion leaves out: the laborer in the factory. Then, he restores the ignominies of the exploitation of labor to the picture. Suddenly, in his ironic characterization, market freedom seems as "spiritual," as unreal, and as irrelevant as Absolute Spirit, and Marx treats it, too, as an illusion.[9]

Marx seems constitutionally incapable of doing what he believes Hegel would like him to do: of "rising to a vision of the whole" that is achieved by making some of the parts—Jews, workers, the labor process—invisible. We can recognize this attitude as consonant with Marx's ontology, which we have understood as sharing its key dynamics with traditional Jewish thought. In both Marx and the Torah, human beings must act, and not just think, in order to make the world right. In both, the aim is for real, practical solutions to the felt needs of concrete human beings, and not for ideal solutions to the imagined problems of purely theoretical people. Reading Marx side by side with Hegel is like comparing Hebrew with Greek—at least, if we read Hegel the way Marx does.

But this brings us back to the question: how does Marx read Hegel? For, after all, Marx does purport to be performing some kind of operation on Hegel's writings. If he arrives at Jewish conclusions, that should make us all the more curious to know how he gets there from where he starts. If Marx is not standing Hegel on his feet, then what is he doing to him? And where does Jewish thought enter into it?

We can readily tell what Marx is not doing. He is not saying, "Hegel is all wrong. He's too Greek. Let's dispense with him." Nor is he saying, "Hegel has corrected the faults of the Greeks: let's embrace his theory." Nor yet is he saying that Hegel has most of it right and only needs correction on certain points. In fact, the more we read Marx on Hegel, the more difficult it becomes to sum up Marx's reaction in any simple formula.

Marx seems rather to be responding to bits and pieces of what Hegel wrote, finding opportunities to express his own recurring themes in the course of his commentary. At moments when Hegel leads to Greek-like conclusions, Marx takes issue with him as if it were obvious Hegel had an obligation to avoid those conclusions. He "corrects" Hegel's theory by subjecting it to certain constraints which he feels but Hegel evidently does not. Those constraints, furthermore, arise out of Marx's dialogical view of the world and his Jewish insistence on the necessary effectiveness of the real.

Where does Marx discover this strange procedure? We are unlikely ever to know for sure. How can we make sense of the way Marx reads and writes, the way he addresses texts, which is the way he develops his theory? Once again, Marx tantalizes with his affinity for a facet of the Jewish tradition. We turn to explore the typically Jewish style of hermeneutics known as *midrash* to pursue the resemblance.

II

Midrash means the creative style of textual interpretation developed by the rabbis of Palestine and Babylonia in the third to sixth centuries c.e. At least, that is one of its meanings. Like *Torah*, the term *midrash* expands and contracts, depending on context. Midrash can mean the exegesis of one verse or part of a verse using "midrashic" methods. It may refer to the product of such an exegesis, whether that is a one-sentence gloss or a series of alternative readings of the same bit of text. Midrash also includes book-length anthologies of these shorter *midrashim*, arranged in the order of the verses on which they comment. *Bereishit Rabbah*, for instance, gives all the classic midrash on the book of Bereishit, or Genesis.

When someone speaks of "the Midrash," furthermore, they usually mean the entire body of these midrashic books, as well as the stories they contain. Indeed, it is a common mistake to refer to any folk story that refers to characters or events in the Torah as a midrash. Some of our contemporary literary critics, on the other hand, focus exclusively on the character of midrash as text about text. They use the term to suggest the construction of a piece of writing as a commentary on, or creative misappropriation of, a precursor author's work. They also employ the term *midrash* to point out the belated and allusive nature of all writing, and to encourage its deconstruction.[10]

What ties together this bundle of usages is the activity of doing midrash. The Hebrew root of the word, *drash*, signifies that midrash is about asking, seeking into, demanding, requiring a response, investigating deeply. When a reader does midrash on a text, he or she wants to know more than what each word or sentence says, or what the author intended to say. He or she also goes beyond the historical circumstances of the text's production and the literary art by which it produces its effects. All these points may interest the midrashist, but they do not satisfy on their own. The reader who is doing midrash wants to discover how the text can help her or him to face the problems of everyday life: her or his own personal dilemmas, and the problems of being a Jew, here and now. The midrash-maker seeks in the text a guide to reengaging in dialogue with God. By wrestling with Scripture, however, the reader has already begun to rejoin that relationship.[11] Midrash thus becomes not only a communication about action, but also an action in itself, an effort of recommitment.

In order to understand midrash (and what the person doing midrash is doing), we need to consider again the unique status of the Torah in the Jewish tradition. We have already remarked that the Torah continuously generates the vital themes of Jewish culture. Within that culture, studying the Torah is conceived as trying to find out what God wants us to do, in order to respond. The Torah is not merely the written covenant of the Jewish partnership with God; it is the place and the moment of dialogue.

Any book which can play such an active role in affairs of cosmic significance is no mere book. In the midrash on the first verse of Genesis, the rabbis accord a new status to the Torah: it is the blueprint of creation.

> It is customary that when a human being builds a palace, he does not build it according to his own wisdom, but according to the wisdom of a craftsman. And the craftsman does not build according to his own wisdom, rather he has plans and records in order to know how to make rooms and corridors. The Holy One, blessed be He, did the same. He looked into the Torah and created the world.[12]

Here we find the Torah lifted out of history—even legendary history, such as the revelation at Sinai—and imagined as existing before creation itself, "written with letters of black fire upon a background of white fire," as another rabbinic source put it.[13] The world is created according to a ground plan which we can discover in the Torah. Hence, say the rabbis who brought midrash to an art, if you want to know anything about the world, look first in the Torah: "Learn it and learn it, for everything is in it."[14] Even and perhaps especially if what you want to understand is not mentioned explicitly in the pages of Scripture, the masters of midrash counsel redoubling your ingenuity. Between the lines, they assure, you will find an answer that will guide you and not mislead.

To be completely relevant, a text must be completely meaningful, too. The rabbis called the Torah an ocean of meaning into which they could plunge again and again without ever plumbing its depths. At the same time, they assumed categorically that every detail of the text—not only its propositions but also the order of the sentences, the repetition or omission of words, the shapes and numerical values of the Hebrew letters, and even the microscopic flourishes of the traditional calligraphy—held important messages for the resourceful reader. *Nothing by chance* could have been their motto. In fact Rabbi Akiba, a major teacher of the second century c.e., quoted the biblical verse, "For it [the Torah] is no empty thing from you: it is your life" (Deut. 32:47) and commented, "If it is empty it is on your account, because you do not know how to interpret it."[15] The duty of every male Jew, according to the rabbis, was to pay that account: to devote substantial time to interpreting the Torah, filling its words with meaning that one could then apply to the direction of one's own life.[16]

Now, to the modern eye, there is something paradoxical about the rabbis' attitude toward the Torah. If the Torah is the ground plan for the world, it must state the objective truth, and then how could it ever be meaningless? Akiba's warning seems misplaced. Surely, a people which believes in a divine document would accumulate an authoritative body of interpretation. Turning exegesis into doctrine, it would eliminate the danger that the text would ever stand empty, or indeed, that believers could mistake its meaning.[17]

On the other hand, if the truth of the Torah is subjective, if its meaning is indeterminate until human readers produce that meaning out of their own thoughts and experiences, why search the Torah at all? Why not apply the same energy to thinking about our problems directly, instead of puzzling through archaic language trying to make sense of it all?

To the rabbis, apparently, these were not serious questions, and not because of blind faith, but simply because the questions missed the point. "Learn it and learn it": assuming that every bit of the Torah has meaning (and potentially, many meanings),[18] our knowledge of what it is saying can never exhaust what it has to say. There is always another interpretation. No single reading can ever replace the text, and none ever will, because as time goes on, changes in our particular situations may empower us to recognize something in the text which was closed to us before.

As for the question, why the Torah at all? The rabbis would not respond by asserting the objective truth of the Torah, or even its utility. They would never justify Torah study in terms of some less ultimate end. Interpreting the Torah is maintaining the dialogue with God, which is humanity's purpose. The question the rabbis would resolve by way of midrash was the question that had formed the covenant between God and humankind: "How shall we hallow the world?" The truth of midrash is not in the text, nor is it in the reader, but in the relation of which both are parts.

In midrash, moreover, rabbinic readers filled one part of creation—a central part, its blueprint, the Torah—with meaning. The process of asking was the beginning of the answer. To shirk the task of interpretation, therefore, would not be an assertion of rational autonomy, but a breaking of faith with our divine partner and with one another. The rabbis could think of deserting the text only as a completely irresponsible act.

As if to emphasize the indispensability of human action to the Torah, both as text and as divine medium, the rabbis came up with a second story to explain the Torah's uniqueness. Going by the biblical account of Exodus, the Torah was given to Moses at Mount Sinai in written form. The rabbis announced, however, that in addition to the written Torah, Moses had received an oral Torah at Sinai: a *torah she b'al peh,* an "instruction by word of mouth." This oral Torah he passed on to his successor Joshua, who transmitted it to the elders of the people, and so on, until in rabbinic times it had lodged itself in the rabbis themselves.[19]

The oral Torah was never an esoteric doctrine. The rabbis of the third century and onward spent huge efforts trying to disseminate it among the people, even to make it into the common law.[20] The existence of an oral Torah, however, did imply that whoever read the Bible without its rabbinic commentary read only a fraction of what Judaism had come to consider the entire text. This had the immediate effect of frustrating Christian proselytizers who sought to expose the Torah as an "Old Testament," since the chain of tradition from Sinai showed that the covenant between God and the Jewish people remained intact.[21]

By settling the question of rabbinic authority, however, the doctrine of an oral Torah paradoxically set rabbinic imaginations free to interpret the written text in creative and innovative ways. True, in order to say something new, the midrashist had first to refer to something old.[22] The rabbis mined the entire Bible for prooftexts with which to support their readings, sometimes creating what they themselves called "a mountain hanging by a hair." By these methods, however, it was almost always possible to find support. In the end, the acceptance or rejection of a midrashic interpretation depended on how well it played off the traditional themes to solve a present-day problem. Breathtakingly, the rabbis declared, "All that a serious student will yet expound before his teacher has already been told to Moses at Sinai."[23] By our faithfulness and our hermeneutic zeal, the rabbis declare, we can actually speak for God. Interpretation transcends revelation.

III

Taking advantage of the latitude that the existence of an oral tradition granted, the rabbis who did midrash borrowed from a treasury of exegetical techniques to open the text even wider. Assuming that the Torah is completely meaningful, as the rabbis did, they could ask about the meaning of any irregularity in the text and expect a serious answer. Did a sentence contain a word that could easily have been omitted? The rabbinic readers would want to know why. Did a word appear in two dissimilar passages? They might weave a story to reveal a hidden link. Was there a gap in the narrative that could not be explained in any other way? Into the breach stepped the midrash-makers. They might take advantage of the way biblical Hebrew is written, without vowels or punctuation, to revocalize words or recombine sentences. They might trade on the numerical value of the Hebrew letters to find hints of other messages that would add up to an equal sum. In effect, in order to find meaning, the rabbis allowed themselves to rewrite the text, over and over, secure in the belief that they were doing God's work. "For it is no empty thing from you": the guarantee takes on the force of a command.

Although to the outside reader some of these midrashim may border on the arbitrary, they could not have been produced and would not have been accepted without a series of constraints that made them legitimate interpretations in the Jewish world. (The constraints mentioned here apply primarily to midrash aggadah, the nonlegalistic variety; midrash halakhah has even tighter requirements.)

To begin with, midrash aggadah is conditioned by the text itself. "No text ever loses its plain meaning," the rabbis ruled.[24] However elaborate the lessons one can draw from a biblical verse by midrash, its more straightforward message (relatively speaking) remained; it was never canceled, as in allegory.

Every midrash had to connect itself, even by a long and tenuous chain of ideas, to a verse or several verses of the Torah. Also, no midrash could successfully claim to exhaust the meaning of its text. It is common, in fact, for midrashic anthologies to list a number of readings on a verse, sometimes more than one being attributed to the same source, and to introduce each one simply as "another interpretation."

Beyond the stimulus of the text, however, what really determined the making of midrash and conferred legitimacy on the final products was a set of concerns and preoccupations shared by rabbinic writers and their readers during the Talmudic period. In his study *The Rabbinic Mind*, Max Kadushin calls these organizing themes "value-concepts."[25] Value-concepts are not values as opposed to facts. Nor are they evaluations. Instead, they are the subjects of which a text can treat that make it seem significant to a given set of readers. Kadushin lists the main rabbinic value-concepts as God's justice, God's love (or mercy), the Torah, and the people of Israel. Midrash aggadah mostly addresses these four topics and the relations between them. Another way of saying this, and perhaps a better one, is that when the rabbis would do midrash, they would seek out problems in the text that might have a bearing on one or more of these four themes.

The value-concepts act as a complex, organismic whole that defines to a great extent what it meant to be a Jew during the third to sixth centuries c.e. Both the self and the "special character of the group," according to Kadushin, depended largely on "the transmission of these valuational terms."[26] They were, and still are, a large part of Jewish culture. By pegging interpretation to these themes, therefore, midrashists made sure of their audience, and by building commentary on commentary, they guaranteed their findings a plausibility that mere pronouncements could not attain.

But did the rabbis believe their midrashim? Did their audiences believe them? It depends on what we mean by belief. If believing is being faced with a question about whether some event actually happened and choosing a "yes" response, then most Jews have never believed midrashim—but they never disbelieved them, either. That yes-or-no question rarely troubles them. Kadushin points out that midrash-makers often hear and acknowledge valid objections to their preferred reading and adhere to it anyway. "Such persistence," he states, "surely implies a belief of some kind, but a belief which . . . is just as surely not unqualified."[27]

A receptive attitude toward midrash necessarily involves a state of mind Kadushin calls "indeterminate belief." In modern philosophical terms, to engage a midrash is to bracket questions of truth in order to seek meaning.[28] But then, as we have seen, Jewish thought finds truth *in* meaning, in the way a reading applies to a reader's situation. The midrashist and his or her readers play with the text, sometimes lightheartedly, but with a serious purpose. The stories they foster say something about their real and pressing problems; through midrash, they gain a deeper understanding of why and how to act.

If a belief is implicated here, it is the bedrock belief in the meaningfulness of the Torah and in the activity of interpretation. To believe is to trust.[29] Doing midrash, especially aggadic midrash, is like exploring one's relationship with another person: knowing objective facts about the other may not move the relationship along any further. Through midrash, Jews "get to know" God and the world. They "believe" insofar as they apply the lessons they learn to the living of their own lives. They believe, not in propositions, but in a dialogue in which they and God are partners, a narrative still in the process of coming to a conclusion. Compared to that faith, what importance has the mere truth-value?

IV

It is useful to look at an example of aggadic midrash which James Kugel has analyzed.[30] The text is Psalm 145, one of many Hebrew poems composed acrostically, with each new line beginning with a new letter of the alphabet. The rabbis noticed, however, that no line starts with the letter *nun:* it is omitted from the sequence. Of course, they had to ask why. Rabbi Yohanan gives one explanation: David, the supposed author of the Psalms, knew that in Amos 5:2, the letter *nun* would begin the dire sentence, "She has fallen (*nafelah*) and will no more rise, the virgin of Israel." He therefore left out the *nun* verse in order to avoid referring to this prophecy of downfall. Rabbi Nahman Bar Isaac seconds this opinion, adding that the next verse following the omission provides the antidote: "The Lord lifts up all who are fallen, and straightens up all who are bent."

So far, this is fairly straightforward, for midrash. True, the question is not one most readers would have come up with, but the midrashist is constantly on the lookout for such minutiae. True, the answer Rabbi Yohanan gives makes David, who lived long before Amos, remarkably precognitive. It is a rabbinic dictum, however, that there is "no before or after in Torah."[31] So, one verse can answer a question about another verse wholly disconnected from it.

Rabbi Nahman's addendum, on the other hand, takes the mere fact of juxtaposition to warrant his reading one verse into its neighbor. His interpretation, together with the one it builds on, treats of God's mercy toward the people of Israel, thus relating two value-concepts in an entirely traditional way.

The sages of Palestine, however, offer a more daring reading than either of these Babylonian rabbis, not of Psalm 145, but of the problematic verse of Amos. They redivide the sentence, thus: "She has fallen and will no more—rise, virgin of Israel!"

What this midrash does is to suspend the original question (and the other answer to that question) to focus on the real problem: the catastrophe that has befallen the Jews' relation with God. At the time these rabbis met, Judea was an abject tributary of Rome. Titus had destroyed the Temple in 70 c.e. and carried many Jews off into slavery. A military revolt led by Simon Bar Kokhba in 135 c.e. had also been crushed, dashing the messianic expectations of his followers. Ten of the most prominent rabbis of Palestine had been tortured to death by the Romans. Jerusalem, the capital and holy city, was declared off-limits to Jews. The country as whole had lost much of its population, and for the second time the Jews were dispersed abroad, with no imminent prospects for return. One Jewish sect, the Nazarenes or Christians, had used these disasters as evidence that the relationship between God and the Jewish people had come to an end, and what they asserted, many others feared.

Against this background, consider what the Palestinian sages did and did not do in their midrash on Amos 5:2. They did not argue, as they might have, that Amos's words only applied to the Babylonian Exile (586–510 B.C.E.) of which he had been speaking. Nor did they read "will no more rise" in a relative sense, as "not for a long time," although this, too, would have been possible. They choose not to take "Israel" as the northern kingdom, as differentiated from Judea, although this reading would at least have mitigated the disaster. Above all, unlike their prophetic forerunners, Isaiah and Jeremiah, they refused to rely on God's omnipotence and God's capacity to annul prophecies of doom out of divine love.

Any of these solutions, in order to reassure, would have required from the people their full belief: not only belief in the validity of the interpretation but also, crucially, belief that its message *must* be true, that God would never hide his face forever. But of course, this faith was exactly what was lacking. The rabbis of Palestine chose instead a solution that required only the willing suspension of disbelief, or what Kadushin calls "*indeterminate belief* which, on occasion, can harden and become determinate."[32] Their midrash, although serious, is at the same time darkly comic. It does not need to be accepted, only repeated, over and over, as a good joke often is, until it becomes part of a common culture which laughs in the face of exile. Together with halakhah, midrashic stories such as these gave the Jews the strong social cohesiveness they needed in order to survive in a world whose meaning they no longer understood.

It is this midrashic function of restoring meaning to a chaotic world which we can find renewed when Marx does theory.

V

No one would mistake any writing by Karl Marx for a specimen of the literary genre midrash.[33] Marx is not writing about the Torah; he is commenting on philosophy and political economy. His language is German, French, or English, never Hebrew or Aramaic. He does not steer by the set of value-concepts that Kadushin enumerates: he cares little for God or Israel except as historical examples and curiosities. True, he is passionate for plays on words. At the height of an argument, he often throws a pun at his readers, such as his contention in *The Holy Family* that the Hegelian movement needed to bathe in a "river of fire"— in German, a *Feuer-bach.* These witticisms make Marx's writings memorable, as clever midrashim do for rabbinic texts. Nothing hangs on them, however. Marx's argument can go on perfectly well without them.

There is more to Marx's theory than his argument alone, however. In his manner of doing theory—his activity or practice of theorizing—we find Marx doing something we might well call midrashic. As we have noticed, while Marx creates his own theory, he reads. His writing proceeds as commentary from his reading. Whole notebooks get filled with line-by-line jottings, creating a record of Marx's associations with certain phrases and his caustic rejoinders to others. Marx's published works also display the signs of his method of working through a text. In *Capital* especially, as Louis Althusser has noted, "We find a reader who reads to us, and out loud"[34] from Smith, Ricardo, and other political economists—just as in "On the Jewish Question" he read to us from Bauer, and in his critique of the *Philosophy of Right* and in the *1844 Manuscripts,* from Hegel.

Now, what determines which pieces of Hegel Marx will find significant? If he were constructing an internal critique, trying to show the limitations of Hegel's theory from its own premises, he would pay most attention to the explicit building blocks and junctures of Hegel's argument. If, on the other hand, Marx were simply disagreeing with Hegel, he would refute his opponent's underlying concepts using his own ideas and his own language.

What we find Marx doing when he reads Hegel is neither of these. We do not see him mounting a critique of Hegel from within; we do not discover him ranging a wholly independent argument alongside the existing one. Marx neither follows Hegel nor wholly deserts him. In the famous afterword to *Capital,* Marx makes a curious boast:

> The mystifying side of Hegelian dialectic I criticised nearly thirty years ago, at a time when [the dialectic] was still in fashion. But just as I was working at the first volume of "Das Kapital," it was the

good pleasure of the peevish, arrogant, mediocre [epigones] who now talk large in cultured Germany, to treat Hegel in the same way the brave Moses Mendelssohn in Lessing's time treated Spinoza, *i.e.,* as a "dead dog." I therefore openly avowed myself the pupil of that mighty thinker, and even here and there, in the chapter on the theory of value, coquetted with the modes of expression peculiar to him.[35]

This "coquetting" shows that the mature Marx, for all his materialism and political radicalism, still finds Hegel meaningful. Why? He cannot explain, any more than he could fully express the reasons that he joined with Hegel "nearly thirty years ago."

We can explain the relationship, however, if we allow ourselves to imagine that Marx reads Hegel as if they were engaged in the same activity: making theory by doing midrash. Perhaps, we might say, Marx and Hegel are both interpreting the world, but each is using a different set of value-concepts. Hegel is trying to reconcile the rational and the real, autonomy for the individual and meaning for the cosmos. Marx is responding to another series of demands: practical human needs, as developed through social history.

Hegel is operating out of what Marx would see as a Greco-Christian reality—but Marx thinks Hegel must be working from the premises of Jewish thought. So, when Marx finds thoughts in Hegel that do not belong, at just those points he feels compelled to bring Hegel back to reality, back to the task at hand: the task set by his own, Jewish sense of the real. On this reading, not only is Marx doing midrash, but he presumes Hegel must be doing so, too.

Where do we find Marx "correcting" Hegel in this manner? In his early, fragmentary *Contribution to the Critique of Hegel's "Philosophy of Right,"* his first attempt to work through Hegel in writing, Marx comments on Hegel almost paragraph by paragraph. Over and over, in endless variations, Marx returns to a centrally Jewish theme: the general is no substitute for the particular. We saw insistence on the particular valued as an interpretive skill in midrash aggadah. Jewish legal reasoning, midrash halakhah, also operates with categories built on specific cases, not general principles.[36]

Most important for Marx, however, is the Jewish protest

against a political state which poses as the general itself, the most adequate expression of the Idea as objective reality, and hence as overarching reality. "As if the actual state were not the people," Marx exclaims. "The state is an abstraction. The people alone is what is concrete." In the name of this state, urgent human needs can be explained away as having already been met on a higher level. Marx penetrates the philosophical shell game he believes supports this political chicanery: the assumption that there is a "general" more real than the particulars on which it is founded.

> The dualism consists in the fact that Hegel does not look upon the general as being the actual nature of the actual finite, i.e., of what exists and is determinate, or upon the actual *ens* [being] as the true subject of the infinite.[37]

Marx finds a similar confusion in Hegel's endorsement of monarchy as the correct form for the ideal state. "Democracy is the truth of monarchy; monarchy is not the truth of democracy." The purpose of any state and any constitution, according to Marx, is to realize the human essence and answer human needs. In order to accomplish this, politics must put real, concrete people in charge of their own lives. Hegel places the monarch in charge instead because the monarch represents the nation in general, but Marx charges that the monarch is just one particular being pretending to be the general. Thus, Marx concludes:

> All other *state forms* are definite, distinct, *particular forms of state.* In democracy the *formal* principle is at the same time the *material* principle. Only democracy, therefore, is the true unity of the general and the particular.[38]

Marx is chiding Hegel for "mistakes" that Hegel obviously meant to make, that Hegel would not consider mistaken at all, differences between Hegel and Marx that are constitutive of Hegel's whole theory. What logic can explain Marx's interpretation? What Marx is doing to Hegel would seem a parody of a reading . . . unless Marx is holding Hegel to a set of Jewish standards: the same standards that seem to be holding Marx.

We conclude, then, that Marx "does midrash" on Hegel in three distinct senses. He comments on particular bits of the Hegelian text, demanding that each detail have meaning. He searches for meaning as defined by a Jewish set of value-concepts (in effect making Hegel an unwilling partner in the tradition). And because his standards of significance fit the pattern of Jewish thought, Marx's commentary makes Hegel significant for readers who continue the concerns of the Jewish tradition. German philosophy had sketched a world on which Jewish thought could get no hold. Marx restores the place of Jewish thought within that world, and of the world within Jewish thought—as midrash has always done.

VI

How Marx mediates between the concerns of the group and of the larger society goes unnoticed in most studies, even that of Althusser, who makes Marx's way of reading central to his analysis of *Capital*. Yet Althusser describes how Marx handles the writings of previous economists in a way that, up to a point, sounds very much like doing midrash.[39] Marx, says Althusser, reads Smith and Ricardo *symptomatically*. He finds statements that "sound hollow" and questions which only seem to have meaning when the question of their possibility has been suppressed. He interrogates his texts, seeking for the absent question that will open up a new world of meaning.

The key symptomatic question Marx finds is, "What is the value of labor?" Because political economists and Marx alike assume that labor is the source of all value, this question can only lead to answers about labor-power and not labor itself—about the amount of work an employer can squeeze out of his workers, not the living, breathing workers who are "labor" in the flesh. Althusser traces how Marx fills in the gaps, or "slots," that the political economists created with their unwitting elision of labor and labor-power. He shows Marx reading in order to create new meaning: the theory of exploitation arises on this exact site.

Most midrashlike of all is the fact that, according to Althusser, Marx's theory is constituted by a set of perspectives and demands which exist independently of his subjective insights. The "problematic," as Althusser calls it, is the form in which a thinker's thoughts must be organized in order to be received as valid knowledge. Marx's "immense theoretical revolution" consists in his change of terrain from an empiricist problematic to one in which structural explanations prevail. Like the idea of a tradition, the concept of a problematic indicates that the sources of meaning lie outside any individual consciousness. When Marx sees further than his precursors, according to Althusser, the problematic itself is doing the sighting through him. Similarly, the rabbis who do midrash claim no personal genius: their discoveries were "already told to Moses at Sinai."

The Althusserian reading of Marx does differ from a midrashic reading, however, to the great benefit of the latter. Marx's problematic in *Capital* represents for Althusser a complete rupture with the past—not only with Smith and Ricardo, but with even the young Marx himself. Over a brief span during the years 1845 and 1846, Marx is said to have abandoned his earlier identity as a radical democrat and Feuerbachian humanist and to have plunged himself into the scientific investigation of social practice. The young Marx had been concerned to liberate the human essence. The mature Marx, according to Althusser, saw human beings as bearers of structural relations with no essence or agency of their own.

In terms of biography alone, Althusser's reading is completely implausible. Althusser makes no attempt to explain why the new problematic, dialectical materialism, should arise just at that time, or why it should make its appearance as a crisis in the thought of this particular German-Jewish radical. Marx's transformation is left as a kind of epiphany—this from Althusser, who vehemently refutes what he calls "the religious myth of reading."[40] Ironically, the effect of Althusser's reading is to invoke a kind of Great Man theory of history. Marx revolutionized theory because he was Marx, and Althusser understands that because he is Althusser.[41]

VII

Reading Marx as a midrash-maker spares us these problems while still giving us the opportunity to ask questions about Marx's way of reading and writing—and his Jewishness. But then, we are faced with a paradox. Marx rejects Judaism and adopts philosophy and political economy, all the while studying them as if they were, or should be, the Torah. He demands that they mean something for the story about the world, humanity, and history that his Jewish sense of the real suggests. If they do not pertain, he reinterprets them so that they do. Here is a strange unconscious piety, an unwilling reverence in the midst of secularity and socialism. How can we account for this mixing of worlds, which Marx neither announces nor explains?

In her discussion of modern thinkers influenced by midrash, Handelman describes a tendency she calls "heretic hermeneutics."[42] Writers who work in this mode can simultaneously affirm their identities as moderns and as Jews without completely submitting to either. This Houdini-like maneuver involves a double displacement. First, the writer leaves the world of the Torah behind. Attention shifts. For Freud, psychology, and for Bloom and Derrida, literary theory become the objects of endless investigation. Into these new realms, however, the heretics tote the old demands. Dreams and works of literature are treated, in the words of Freud, "as Holy Writ": in other words, as the Torah. They are expected, even demanded, to be meaningful down to their tiniest detail. The modern critic interprets them as a midrashmaker would do: to make them significant to pursuits he or she believes the text must share.

With Marx, we cannot see the exegetical techniques, but we can sense the gravitational pull that midrash exerts over his writings. "For it is no empty thing from you": Marx attaches himself to Hegel (and then to political economy) because of their tantalizing similarities to the reality in which he believes and which he is struggling to bring to life. These hints of a meaningful world, he cannot ignore. He can never fully accept them, either. At best, he can note them in a spirit of indeterminate belief. Eventually, he must reorder everything, including his own first readings.

"Of course," Marx wrote in an afterword to *Capital,* "the method of presentation must differ in form from that of inquiry."[43] We have already seen that the way Marx presented one central feature of his theory, its relation to that of Hegel, has obscured more than it has helped. Without explaining midrash, Marx could not explain his own activity. Without recognizing the demands his Jewish sense of the real imposed on him, he could only wish and hope to find an audience that would share his value-concepts. Yet, the Jewish terms in which his ontology and his philosophy of writing make sense were foreign to Marx's audience, and to Marx himself. In the next chapter, we will consider how this dilemma affects our reading of Marx's overall project, and how the Jewish theme of exile, retranslated by Marx's theory of alienation, may help us to understand Marx better.

CHAPTER 5

Alienation
as Exile

EVERYTHING Karl Marx ever wrote—philosophy, history, economics, politics—takes aim at the problem of alienation. Overcoming the historical circumstances which have forced some of us to work for others, under their control and for their profit, thus wasting our own creative powers and losing the commodities we end up spawning, the raw materials we might have used, and the wholeness of self and society we need more than anything but life itself: this is Marx's theme and his goal as a theorist.

Alienation is the key-word of Marx's earlier writings, but it appears over and over in *Capital*, too.[1] And well it might. For alienation and the transcending of alienation both require, in Marx's own words, "very palpable, material conditions," and it is to discover the details of those conditions that Marx began his economic research at all.[2]

As crucial as the word *alienation* is to Marx, it has proved equally troublesome to Marxists. First, they have had to defend the term from social psychologists and other researchers who would set it equal to "dissatisfaction."[3] This apparently value-neutral term in fact strips away the whole theory of human needs that gives alienation its meaning. Among Marxists, furthermore, there are those who would resist the language of alienation altogether, preferring the more analytical categories of historical materialism.[4] Their choice weights the scales in favor of a deterministic reading of Marx, which sits poorly with Marx's Jewish emphasis on the importance of human action.

A third problem arises in humanist Marxism, which casts the

distortions of the self and of social relations produced by capitalism as mere objects of protest, examples of "man's inhumanity to man." At its most basic, the humanist approach underestimates the power of economic and institutional barriers to human freedom, something that Marx never did.[5]

We should not be misled by this multiplicity of partial readings. None of his followers has deserted Marx's struggle against alienation completely. As Alasdair MacIntyre acutely observes: "When a tradition is in good order it is always partially constituted by an argument about the goods the pursuit of which gives to that tradition its particular point and purpose."[6] By this standard, the debate over alienation may even be a sign of Marxism's continuing good health despite apparent reversals in Europe. As long as the place of alienation in Marxism still matters to the participants, the tradition goes on.

Yet, as MacIntyre also suggests, sometimes an argument loses touch with what it is about, and a tradition "gets interpreted and misinterpreted in terms of the pluralism which threatens to submerge us all."[7] Some readings of Marx's theory of alienation do let us learn more, and some differently than others. Faced with the necessity to choose among interpretations, we should ask: what version will help us understand the urgency with which Marx confronts alienation? For alienation is no abstract problem to Marx: it is more like an obsession. What can we do to feel that obsession the way Marx did? Since otherwise, we shall be hard put to say we have understood it at all.

Where shall we search for an understanding of alienation's profound influence on our lives as described in Marx's theory? Let us begin by ignoring the ongoing debate on the subject, and let us continue by setting aside for the moment Marx's own writings on alienation. Marx did not provide us with the full context we needed in order to understand his midrash on Hegel. We may also suspect that when he writes about alienation, he is not pausing to explain what he is doing. We shall have to imagine that for ourselves. So, we shall approach alienation circuitously, edging up to it from an entirely unexpected direction. We shall explore the meaning of alienation via a midrash on the theme of exile.

I

The text we are examining is the first line of the book of Bereishit, or Genesis. We are accustomed to the translation which reads, "In the beginning God created the heavens and the earth. Now the earth was formless and void. . . ."

The Torah, however, is written without vowels or punctuation; hence, many interesting possibilities unfold. An equally valid reading would have Genesis 1:1–2 say: "When God began to create the heavens and the earth, the earth became (*hayta*) formless and void."[8] Now, long ago, in the sixteenth century C.E., Rabbi Isaac Luria, called the Lion, read the verse in just this manner. And here is the story he told:

> Before Creation, God filled infinity. There was no dot of space, no instant of time, which was not part of the divine. In order to create the world—because God was lonely—God had first to make room, to withdraw from infinity and to contract within the divine self.
>
> So, the first thing created was the empty space, the nothing, the "formless and void." Into this absence, God emanated pure God energy. It was like a river of light pouring, liquid, into containers also made of light.
>
> But the freely flowing emanation could not contain itself. The vessels shattered. The shards fell into chaos. And the scraps of the broken vessels came to encase the light they had held like scars over wounds, like thick, woody shells over nuts.[9]

All that we now recognize as our world, said Luria and his followers, is really the jumble that resulted from the shattering of the vessels. The world is infinitely precious: every bit contains sparks of the divine. But just for that reason, it is direly in need of repair. The Lurianic *Kabbalah* (or mystical tradition) heralds this crisis by stating that when the primordial vessels shattered, at that same moment God's imminent presence, called the *Shekhinah*, went into exile.

The Shekhinah is exiled here with us in this reality, which is the only reality, but which is tragically unlike what it should be. We are called, the Kabbalists would say, to redeem the sparks of divine light by hallowing every being. And they would begin every religious act (which could include sitting down to a meal, or putting on clothes) with the declaration, "This is done for the sake of reuniting God and His Shekhinah." What has been fragmented will be made whole; what has been exiled will return.

Like any good midrash, Rabbi Luria's picks up themes from the
traditional account and deepens them in surprising ways. The
story of the shattering of the vessels makes human action absolutely crucial in the universe. It underlines God's dependence on
humanity. Not only do we determine the success or failure of
divine purposes: we must heal the divine being. God is constituted in relation to us, and the predicament which imposes
God's needs sets us our task as well. Furthermore, that task
concerns itself with our day-to-day existence and the practical
details of material life. All this is traditional; it fits easily with
what was "told to Moses at Sinai."

Yet Luria's tale also revises traditional Jewish thought in a
drastic way. In the Torah, "the Lord is near to all who call upon
Him," and "this Instruction," God's voice in the dialogue, is "in
your mouth and in your heart, to do it" (Exodus 30). We find no
mention of God's purposes gone awry, no indication that we need
to know anything that preceded the world in order to hallow it. In
the Torah, creation is unfinished because it is ongoing; in the
Kabbalah, because it is broken off.

Thus, the exile of the Shekhinah is a catastrophic event which
disrupts cosmic purposes and makes reality ironic. It requires
our unrelenting effort to effect its reversal, to bring God's presence and ourselves home from exile. Short of that return, the
Kabbalah suggests, we cannot know our true purposes, and we
cannot be whole. Return and the longing for return become life's
content. In the absence of dialogue, the need to restore dialogue
establishes what it means in Judaism to be a person.[10]

I want to propose that Marx's theory of alienation shares the
basic movements of the story of exile and return we find in Luria.
Taking the true weight of alienation into account, we shall have
to revise our understanding of Marx's ontology, too, just as Luria's
midrash on exile at creation rewrote the Torah's themes of dialogue and partnership with God.

All these convergences will become more evident, however, if we
go back to examine other Jewish texts in which the theme of exile
is at work. As we noted earlier, in the Torah each recurrence of a
theme must be read backwards and forwards as a commentary on
every other episode which it informs. We shall discuss three biblical examples which, although they pertain to events in history

and not before it, weave exile and return into their narratives.[11] Next, as a kind of summation, we shall do our own midrash on a verse from a twentieth-century Jewish poet. Then and only then shall we be ready to discuss Marx's theory of alienation in the framework of exile.

II

Luria's midrash tells us how exile affects God and the cosmos. The story of the expulsion of Adam and Eve from the Garden of Eden shows how human beings suffer exile, too. But in order to learn that particular lesson we need first to forget the Christian reading of Eden with which, since John Milton, we have become familiar. That story speaks not of exile but of "Adam's fall." It postulates that the sin of eating from the forbidden tree revealed the inherent sinfulness of human nature, which manifested itself again directly in Adam's and Eve's descent into sexuality from what is assumed was their previous spiritual plane.

Jewish readers have interpreted this story very differently. In the midrash on Genesis 2–3, disobedience, not sexuality, is the sin for which Adam and Eve are banished. Sexuality is recognized to be fraught with moral dangers, but it is also a positive commandment: "Be fruitful and multiply, and replenish the earth" (Genesis 1:28). Moreover, at least one midrashist claims that the serpent found Eve alone because Adam had "engaged in his natural functions [an idiom for intercourse] and then fallen asleep."[12] Clearly, on this reading, sexuality was not a *consequence* of the serpent's temptation.

Beyond that, Martin Buber questions the notion that sin, or "a decision between good and evil," is the topic of the story at all. Instead, he argues, Adam and Eve decide for the *knowledge* of good and evil, "adequate awareness of the opposites latent in creation."[13] Arthur Waskow goes on to wonder whether leaving Eden was not a punishment but a necessary step toward maturity—less like the shattering of the vessels and more like that initial contraction by which, in Luria's story, God prepared for the creation of the world.[14] This reading seems to contradict the text, but it shows how far from, say, Milton's Eden the Jewish commentator feels free to go.

Since we are not, at any rate, compelled to read the story of the expulsion as a lesson about sexuality and original sin, we are free to ask what we can learn from it about exile. Adam and Eve, we are told, were driven forth from the Garden. This exile transformed their lives and those of their descendants so much that an angel with a flaming sword poised at the outskirts of Eden is an apt symbol of the impossibility of their going on unchanged (Genesis 3:24). We should be asking, then, about the consequences of the expulsion. How does exile affect human lives? What did Adam and Eve lose when they left Eden behind?

The Torah mentions four changes that confronted the first couple when they departed from the Garden. They became ashamed before each other and before God. They had to work hard and unrelentingly in order to survive. Even "in the sweat of thy brow," they could never be sure of producing what they needed to live: the earth, from which they sprang, became their adversary. Finally, the sexual relation and the act of giving birth became bound up with pain and travail.

All the activities that human beings had enjoyed in Eden as partners in creation, they now find themselves doing under the whip of necessity. The most basic human needs, food, labor, and love, can only be met sporadically, uncertainly, in a way that denies humanity's responsibilities as namers and tenders of the world. For Adam and Eve, exile means that a sense of estrangement has filtered into their dialogue with God, affecting both God and human. It cannot be willed away, only struggled with and gradually, painfully transcended.

But humanity decides to try for a shortcut. Instead of learning how to be human in order to become God's partners once again, they opt to become gods themselves. On the plain of Shinar, the tower went up, story after story, an assault on the heavens. Building the tower of Babel was a truly monumental effort, spurred on by an equally great fear: "lest we be scattered abroad upon the face of the whole earth" (Genesis 11:4). Ironically, by their own actions, the builders provoked the fate they feared. The Torah tells that God "did there confound the language of all the earth." None of them could understand each other. Their common purpose lost, they scattered. Their exile was complete with the fragmenting of their shared speech; after that, physical dispersal was all but a foregone conclusion. The tower builders had lost sight of God's purposes in creating human beings who could act, and so they lost, too, the ability to frame common purposes of their own, of any sort, from Babel onward.

Hence it is the people of Israel and not polyglot humanity who carry the burden of repairing the world during most of the biblical story. That nation suffers exile twice—once in biblical times— with the successive destructions of the Temple first by the Babylonians in 586 B.C.E. and then in 70 C.E. by the Romans. In both instances, not only do the Jews become captives, uprooted from their land, but they also undergo the destruction of the legal and cultural institutions that had housed everyday Jewish life. Many of the 613 *mitzvot*, or commandments of the Torah, could not be carried out anywhere but in the land of Israel. Others had no applications in the climates and social structures that the exiles began to inhabit, while still others made sense only as directives to a self-governing people.

With good reason, then, the Jews of the Diaspora asked, "How shall we sing the Lord's song in a strange land?" Like Eve and Adam, they had all they could do to keep themselves alive on alien and hostile soil. Like the shocked crowd at Babel, they were forced both figuratively and literally to speak in new languages which blocked the expression and even the memory of what they had been working at before. And when they swore, "If I forget thee, O Jerusalem, let my right hand lose its cunning," they underscored the tacit truth that henceforth, Jerusalem might live as the capital of Jewish life only in memory.

III

Memory, and the language which preserves it, have become a matter of life and death for Jews in exile. As Harold Bloom writes, "Jewry can survive without a Jewish language . . . but not without language, not without an intense, obsessive concern that far transcends what we ordinarily call literacy."[15] Gestures and rituals have the power to stir something nameless within, and sometimes, to evoke an unspoken meaning that, like a tradition, gives people their bearings for a little while. But in exile, what is last to give way as the institutional foundations of identity crumble is language: for Jews, the discursive structures of dialogue. No matter what Jews know or accept of their religion, when they address the demand to hallow the world through material action guided by changing human needs, they return to the situation which seems most real to them and in which they feel most right to themselves.

Language helps create a meaningful world—or destroy it. One aspect of exile is losing one's own voice, having to use terms and concepts that others recognize and address problems that others deem significant in order to say anything, even indirectly, about what concerns one most. Then one route to return from exile would be to speak in a voice one can claim as one's own: to tell the story of one's estrangement, one's present needs, and one's stuttering attempts to reshape the world into a home—to tell the story . . . and to attract an audience which has the language, the empathy, and above all, the good will to hear.

As our final midrash on the theme of exile, therefore, let us try to listen to someone who is trying to be heard. American Jewish poet Charles Reznikoff writes:

> How difficult for me is Hebrew:
> even the words for *mother*, for *bread*, for *sun*
> are foreign. How far have I been exiled, Zion.

"How difficult for me is Hebrew." This opening sentence, to anyone who has been a student, calls up a sensation which is all too familiar. Someone is working hard at learning, in this case a language, without having any real aptitude for it. Many of us know how that feels. We can shake our heads ruefully and sympathize. But: this man is a Jew. The language he is trying to learn is his own language. How can we comprehend that?

For just a moment, imagine yourself suddenly forgetting how to speak English. You have to express yourself now, say, in German, in words that seem strange and disconnected, in a grammar you learned out of a textbook. Not only do you have to search for words when you try to talk with other people; in your own mind, you hear yourself in an alien tongue.

Can you feel that? The constant groping for vocabulary, the

unsureness that you have said what you meant to say, or that what you said made sense, the biting scorn or condescending patience of the others toward this half-wit foreigner? "Difficult," the poet says. "Difficult" is not the word for your situation.

But think instead that this loss of yours did not happen yesterday but a long time ago, a lifetime ago—in fact, as far back as you can remember. You are unaware that you ever spoke another language. Only, there are these gaps in conversation where you know you want to say something but cannot figure out what, only that it is important. So, you try anyway, hoping to reach someone with a piece of it, a hint, a spark. To your amazement, your neighbors hear only what they expect to hear. The mold of their common understandings keeps casting your tentative, hopeful messages back in to the same distorted shape. Do you rage at their obtuseness? Or blame yourself for this vague something you cannot seem to say? This is a dimension of exile: losing your own thoughts to a foreign language.

"Even the words for *mother*, for *bread*, for *sun* / are foreign." Why these words? Why not bigger, meatier words like *freedom*, *power*, *Spirit*, or, for that matter, *alienation*? The poet feels estranged precisely from the everyday. If he knew his own language, through interpretation the tiniest, most personal elements of his life would become sources of meaning and chances to respond. Because the terms of his intimate existence are foreign to him, the poet finds them "difficult," not as a problem is difficult but as a person is: obstreperous, obstructionist, perversely resisting what is obvious and what has to be done, which is none other than the hallowing of the world. Obvious, it is no longer. How can it be, when everyone and everything, including the language he speaks, insist that it cannot be done? This is a second dimension of exile: when your own needs seem foreign, and the difficulty of an integrated life confronts you like an enemy.

The poet seeks his own language, his own needs, and even his own land. "How far have I been exiled, Zion": the hill country of Judea is the terrain of Jewish memory. But exile is not a matter of geography alone. This thick-witted Hebrew student could move to Jerusalem tomorrow and be worse off, not better. His problem, we read, is not land but life. The State of Israel is not Zion. In Zion, "the words for *mother*, for *bread*, for *sun*" would be spoken in a living communal effort to discover how to do that for which we are. No state we know can do that. No country has ever been Zion.

Is this too paradoxical, the poet's longing to return to a place he has never been? On the contrary. How can his need be silent until it is fulfilled? Zion is not an abstraction. To him, it is no completely rational society inhabited by two-dimensional figures. Zion is what he is longing for with his blood and heart and bones. Even now, perhaps, he is sometimes there: not in a blinding flash, but in the sound of a still, small voice that whispers to him what his words might mean. He is *called* back. And his return becomes real, and he starts to live a real life. Following a poignant phrase of Marx's, he begins to make his poetry out of the future.

But ever and again, he finds out how far his exile has carried him. The familiar landmarks have shifted; it is no good, trying to steer by them now. His pleas fall on empty air. He is suddenly a man alone, having trouble with his language lessons, while all around him float the shibboleths of a country which is inescapably, inexcusably foreign. Being in exile, then, means trying to sing the Lord's song in a strange land.

But this brings us to a fourth dimension of exile, one that Reznikoff only hints at, so that we will need the fine reading skills of midrash in order to discover it. When the poet says, in the first line, "How difficult for me is Hebrew," he is speaking in soliloquy, a form which heightens the sense of isolation his words express. By the third line, however, he changes his mode of address. He employs apostrophe, a figure in which the person addressed is not literally there. "How far have I been exiled," he says, "Zion." Now, what of it? Is there anything here that adds to our understanding of exile, beyond simply concluding that the poet knows his trade?

"Zion." The apostrophe calls into play someone who is not there even when *there* means "in the words of the poem." It speaks to someone whose name the poet never utters. For "Zion" cannot be the one meant to hear. Zion is a place, a condition for the task, but not a partner in it. The poet is reaching out metonymically to someone for whom his difficulty matters. To whom is the poet speaking?

When, throughout history, Jews have found themselves challenged by the need to integrate all aspects of their lives and to dedicate them to the fulfillment of the world, and when, so choosing and having been chosen, they asked how they should begin, they traditionally named the one they questioned, God. The name, however, is unimportant. What matters, to Judaism and to this Jewish poet, is the act of questioning, which thrusts the questioner into the middle of a relationship based on a shared predicament.

This entering into dialogue is the beginning of an exile's return. It is only a beginning—for the poet is still a stranger in a strange land. But if the movement of dialogue impels him to build the community he calls Zion, it will enable him little by little to feel at home in the world. The dialogical relation makes a home for him because it establishes the structure of self, group, and world on which his identity depends.

IV

The stories of exile we have just explored, from Luria's to Reznikoff's, plumb the meaning of exile more deeply than any definition can do. The text of the Torah, we remarked earlier, is its own best summary. In the same way, the stories which introduce us to the theme of exile also provide our models of the situation. No description or exposition can do as well, for none can reproduce in us the emotional response which is vital to knowing exile from within. We were able, however, to detach certain motifs from the Torah narrative for their pertinence to our current inquiry, and we can do the same with our stories of exile. Let us carefully direct our attention to some of the more broadly applicable features of exile, aspects we may recognize again in the lineaments of Marx's theory of alienation.

We can think of exile in two distinct but intrinsically related ways. Exile may be the burden of some particular social group, or it may be the condition of a whole society, affecting all its individual members.

In the first sense, we can specify that exile touches only certain kinds of groups within a society. We would not expect to apply it in describing the group of left-handed people, or redheads, Democrats, or Virginians. Exile occurs only to groups which share more existentially basic situations, so that the defining characteristics of the group also structure the selves of its members. Most likely, a group in exile will possess some shared purpose or task, the elaboration and continuous interpretation of which is a central element in the way the group is constituted. Exile, then, affects people in relation to how their identities depend on situations or purposes shared in common within a group.

Again, we can stipulate that a group which finds itself in exile (in the first sense) is never the dominant force in society. One of the important ways in which exile manifests itself is in the relation of the exiles to the dominant group and to the parameters of the self it maintains for the whole society. We might therefore propose that some group (for example, the Jews) is in exile with respect to the society which it inhabits (say, nineteenth-century Germany) as a result of some factor or factors. Those factors have to do with the self created by the task or situation which partially defines the group, that task or situation not being constitutive of the host society in general.

Both from our stories and our analysis, it is already clear that even a profound difference need not be an exile. What can put a subordinate social group partially constituted by a task or situation into an exiled state? Primarily, it is how the group diverges from the mainstream in the way its members construct reality. Simply by responding to their task, exiled groups tacitly employ categories of meaning and standards of significance which others do not use or recognize.

The exiles themselves may be aware of the incongruity, or they may not, and whether they are will have little bearing on whether their deviant sense of the real becomes a problem for them. If their group lives separate from society, interacting with the larger culture mainly for instrumental purposes, then they can maintain their understanding of self and reality with little strain. (The ghetto-dwelling Jews of premodern Europe were an example.)[16] If, however, the group lives in and among its neighbors, partakes of their culture, and permits its members to pursue goals extraneous to its existential task, yet still forms its members so that they must respond to that task, then the scene of a tragic conflict is set.

The members of such a group as we have been describing (and modern Jews, I contend, are such a group) are forced to know the world and conduct themselves in society on the basis of two differing conceptions of reality: that of the group, and that of the surrounding culture. Both realities are their own. The individual's identity is incomplete unless he or she can somehow manage to make sense of himself or herself as an actor in both situations. Yet a world in which one is called to do a certain task may be at odds with a world which demands another direction to one's efforts. It is almost certainly irreconcilable with a nation of the world that gives people no purposes at all, but only arbitrary and contingent desires.

Now, at this point, the people in this group are in exile. They lack an ontology which accepts *all* their concerns as real, as well as a language adequate to express those concerns. Consequently, they cannot express their constitutive purposes and needs, either to outsiders or to each other. They have lost the shared context of meaning which makes interpreting even one's own experience possible. They are impeded from formulating their experience, even to themselves.

The relation between the exiles and their neighbors is not symmetrical. Most citizens of a society possess a language and an ontology sufficient to their needs. They can make themselves understood by each other and by the exiles, and in general, they have the privilege to know when they are making sense; that is, when their statements and claims will be taken seriously, with a good chance of securing agreement. On those rare occasions when other members of a society do not make sense to the exiles, it is the exiles and not society who are believed to have failed—in society's judgment, and usually in their own.

For the exiles, the discursive norms of their society are the flaming sword barring their way home. They can only enter the "garden of being taken seriously" by leaving important parts of themselves behind. And this continues to be true as long as they are in any way part of the group, until they have completely forgotten their specific situation and task.

The exile that affects specific groups is more than a malaise of discourse: it is the fingerprint of power. We can see power at work in the silencing of the exiles about their unique experience, the excluding of their difference from what society counts as real, and the very act of producing the exiles as people who must give a rational account of themselves and cannot. Power operates at the same time to estrange the exiles from themselves, from each other, and from other human beings. The social relations in which they seek fulfillment are fraught with tensions, instead.

Exile also extends into the realm of political processes. The particular group which is exiled cannot use the procedures of liberal democracy to address its needs: first, because it cannot formulate them; second, because many of them deal with what are called "private" matters; third, because the language of rights, interests, and utility cannot justify them; and fourth, because by admitting themselves unable to fit the narrow confines of the rational individual, the exiles declare themselves unfit to participate in public life.

So far, we have spoken of exile only in the first sense, as it affects particular groups in a society. We have outlined it as a breakdown in the normal, equal relations between members of those groups and all other individuals. Implicit in that definition, however, is another understanding of exile, one that designates a condition which could affect the whole of a society.

Let us assume, as both Marx and the Jewish tradition do, that humanity shares not a common end, predetermined, but a common purpose. Let us further assume that pursuing this purpose requires the active development of our human powers. Any society which fails to make this task its center runs the risk of becoming an obstacle to a good human life. It matters naught whether the purpose which makes us human is crystallized as hallowing the world or realizing human powers, or as love, brotherhood or sisterhood, community, or spiritual nobility. In pursuing any of these, the individuals who live in a society which ignores human purposes will be hindered, simply because they cannot rely on one another.

In some cases, a society which bears this second kind of exile will lack not only a purpose, but also any notion of common purpose, or of why such a shared project might be worthwhile. If a group in exile of the first sort inhabited a society of exile in the second meaning, the estrangement of self, group, and social whole would have reached its ultimate crazy peak.

V

We can read Marx's theory of alienation as an attempt to capture in words the plight of an exiled group in a society without purpose: namely, the workers under capitalism. The reality of the proletariat, Marx argues, is structured by its members' deep and abiding need for creative work. This need is generated by the task to which Marx believes all human beings are drawn, but in which the working class, of all segments of society, is most frustrated: the realization of their human powers. Workers, Marx contends, feel the pull of this aspect of themselves as something tangible, and they suffer from not being able to pursue it.

> What constitutes the alienation of labor? First, that the work is *external* to the worker, that it is not part of his nature; and that, consequently, he does not fulfill himself in his work, but denies himself, has a feeling of misery rather than well-being, does not develop freely his physical and mental energies but is physically exhausted and mentally debased.[17]

The misery Marx describes is partly the result of exploitation. In his famous chapter of *Capital* on "The Working Day," he serves an indictment of capitalism for laying waste the lives of the workers with long hours and brutal conditions.[18] Primarily, however, we find Marx attacking the evils of alienation itself: not the loss of hours or things, but the catastrophe of capitalism for human relations. Alienated labor, writes Marx, disrupts the self, insofar as it prevents the workers from fulfilling their task as species-beings, which is essential to who they are. By the same token, it takes away their common purpose by denying it any social importance. As its end product, too, alienated labor reproduces a class system and a mode of production which allow no room and provide no resources for the workers to develop in any direction that does not boost profit and productivity.[19]

If we say, then, that the working class is in exile within capital-

ist society because its sense of the real requires it to do what
capitalism makes impossible, we will have gone a long way toward showing why the transcending of alienation is what Marx
cares about most. Interpreted as exile, alienation is more than an
injustice: it is a tragedy. It deprives workers of the ability to make
sense of their world. Without that ability, none of their other
powers matters.[20]

But not only the workers are alienated. In *The Holy Family*,
Marx writes:

> The propertied class and the class of the proletariat present the
> same human self-alienation. But the former class finds in this self-
> alienation its confirmation and its good, its own power: it has in it
> a semblance of human existence.[21]

Within the capitalist scheme of things, the bourgeoisie holds all
the advantages. As Ollman observes, however, these privileges
"concern registering a higher score on a scale which must itself
be condemned."[22] The capitalists are no more free than the workers to pursue their human task. They, too, inhabit a world in
which commodities and money rule the use of human energy,[23]
and labor is treated as a source of a mysterious good called "value"
instead of as an intrinsic human activity.[24] Workers and capitalists both conduct their lives according to the variations of the
market. Its boom-and-bust cycle, and not their own needs and
powers, supplies the situation to which they respond and which
they search for meaning. We can summarize this general crazi-
ness, this inversion of human reality,[25] by saying that Marx portrays capitalism as a society in exile. In order for us to become
free, that exile must end.

Reading alienation as an analogue to exile, we understand why
it is Marx's overriding concern. We also begin to appreciate the
cruel irony that alienation inflicts on us, according to Marx. Exile
takes the challenge of hallowing the world in dialogue—which
already demands our every effort—and adds to it the agonies of
separation, changing the joys of partnership in creation to the
numbing struggle for existence. Likewise, alienation distances
us from our own powers and our own needs. It makes our immediate sense of what to do, unreliable; our apperception of the real,
ambivalent; and our basis for joint action, contingent and unpre-

dictable. Neither exile nor alienation stifles the call that moves us to realize our task. Both, however, muffle its volume and baffle our attempts to respond.

If that is so, however, then Marx finds himself in a very serious dilemma as a theorist and as a revolutionary. Based on the view of Marx's ontology we took in chapter 3, he should strive to use his theory to bring his neighbors back to an awareness of their still-unmet needs. He should explain how the social structures under which they are laboring have limited their humanity and stultified their consciousness, and he should move them to revolutionize the mode of production in all its social ramifications.

The theory of alienation, however, suggests that people's acceptance of their "particular situation" in "the present enslaved world" is not a mistake, but a loss of meaning. Capitalism shapes human beings. It may "make us so stupid," but it makes us, nevertheless. Marx is caught in a bind. People who are well and truly alienated will not respond to his call to shape a more human world. They will deny that the world can be human, for that is what it means to be alienated.

To have the effect Marx hoped for, his theory would have to find an audience which believed in the continuing force of unmet human needs, which took the answering of them as an imperative, and which refused to accept spiritual solutions as real satisfaction. He would have to reach people who could balance the pressing demands of the present capitalist system with their allegiance to an absent but humanly necessary order. Marx's theory requires adherents who can mount a revolution (because they must), then strive together to accomplish tasks about the need for which they maintain a sense of humor, in a spirit of indeterminate belief. To become fully human, he must rely on people who can be more human than their society permits.

Perhaps—just perhaps—we could fulfill Marx's project if we knew our situation was exile. Perhaps if we longed to return, we could. But no one in Marx's society lived life every day as a story of exile and return. Marx himself did not. He only wrote as if he did.

Conclusion: Political Discourse in Exile

Then it will transpire that the world has long been dreaming of
something that it can acquire if only it becomes conscious of it.
It will transpire that it is not a matter of having a great dividing
line between past and future, but of carrying out the thoughts of
the past. And finally, it will transpire that mankind begins no
new work, but consciously accomplishes its old work.—Karl
Marx

AT THE BEGINNING of this essay, we set out to
explore the relation between Marx's Jewishness and the structures of his political theory. Marx's philosophy of writing, with its
invitation to find meaning in the gaps of his own written work,
gave us our provisional charter. We asked, What Jewish patterns
of thought reappear to us in the movement of Marx's theory? How
would Marx make more sense—or a different, more interesting
sense—if we read him as a writer in the Jewish tradition?

Now, we can summarize what we have found.

Reading through and beyond what Marx actually wrote, we
discover that Jewish patterns of thought offer an intriguing perspective on Marx's project. Biblical ontology, for instance, helps
bring out the distinctive features of Marx's sense of the real,
which we find not so much in his political and economic doctrines as in his presumptions about the world, the thinker, and
the relations between them. Like the Torah, Marx does not con-

ceive of reality as that which merely is. Nor does he locate human
excellence in seeing reality as it is in its essence. Instead, he
outlines a theory in which human beings help to constitute the
world through their actions.

Moreover, in Marx's theory, people act out of a sense of need
which previous human actions have helped to create and which
continue to evolve throughout history. This dialectic of needs insures that reality—human, social reality—will continue to
change, too. Therefore, no thinker can stand outside the currents
of history and declare the truth, once and for all. In order to interpret the world, the philosopher must contribute to changing it.

With this conception, Marx deliberately sets himself apart from
the classical Greek philosophers and from most modern theorists
as well. To him, all these thinkers seem to be searching for eternal
and universal truths about human nature. At best, they admit
the reality of social change only as progress toward a fixed and
highest end. Their chosen perspective is that of the detached
observer and the disinterested seeker of wisdom. Marx regards
this entire line of thought as ideology. His own narrative and
dialogical idea of history allows him to study actual, particular
changes in human needs and the capacity of society to meet those
needs. It also gives him the critical force to demand political
struggle in order to win human freedom, the freedom to answer
the needs that continue to rise and challenge human beings in
history.

As Marx distances himself from the Greco-Christian canon, he
approaches the standpoint of the Jewish tradition. Unlike the
Torah, Marx's theory has no use for God: Marx relocates all needs
and all capacities within species *homo sapiens* itself. But an
important effect of his so doing is to free human beings from the
"God's-eye viewpoint" that glances past material oppression to
find purely spiritual solutions. Like the Hasidic rabbi Moshe Leib
of Sasov, Marx refuses to put off the needy with pious words; in
the face of suffering, they both say, "You shall act as if there were
no God, as if there were only one person in all the world who could
help"—only yourself. [1]

In his stress on the indispensability of human action, Marx
echoes the Jewish motifs of *partnership in Creation* and *di-*

alogue. He takes the imperatives of the Jewish situation as they resound in the Torah and transposes them into those of the species.

This insistent introduction of Jewish themes appears to us again when we examine closely how Marx treats Hegel. No simple inversion model explains what Marx does to the Hegelian dialectic. He challenges, corrects, and revises it at the key points where it departs from the Jewish understanding of reality. It is just as if Marx were holding Hegel responsible for addressing Jewish concerns, a responsibility he never explicitly takes on himself.

Studying the rabbinic mode of textual interpretation called *midrash,* however, we can form a better idea of what Marx is doing here. Like a midrashist, Marx, reading Hegel, excerpts significant points and passages on which to comment. He tries to make the earlier writer speak to his own preoccupations (his "value-concepts," as Kadushin would say). Marx interprets as if any text he reads must necessarily have meaning for him and his particular questions. The rabbis of the Talmudic period, who assumed the divinity of their text, did the same. Furthermore, we see Marx breathing new life into Hegel through his reinterpretation, making Hegel's texts a necessary corridor by which to reach his own. As Lenin wrote in 1914:

> It is impossible completely to understand Marx's *Capital,* and especially its first chapters, without having thoroughly studied and understood the whole of Hegel's *Logic.* Consequently, half a century later none of the Marxists understood Marx.[2]

Indeed, understanding Marx must have been a nightmare for his colleagues and contemporaries. Our findings suggest that to appreciate what Marx was doing, Marx's readers would have to employ Hegelian dialectics, biblical ontology, and midrashic ingenuity, all at once. Compared to the classics of Western thought, all Marx's writings (and not just the *Grundrisse,* as Martin Nicolaus claims) are "altogether unique and in every sense strange product[s] of the intellect, and must have appeared like reflections of some man from a different planet."[3] Yet Marx labored over these writings, and he clearly meant most of them to be read. Hence, we confront the paradox of a man striving energetically to communicate with an audience that is nowhere at hand.

Once more, it is the Jewish tradition which hints at the possibility of such an estrangement. The theme of exile portrays the breakdown of meaning between self, situation, and other that recurrently plagues a people which is partially constituted by a compelling purpose. When changes in the world they inhabit make the tasks pertaining to such a group impossible to fulfill, its members suffer. They are injured in their identity, in their claim to social resources that they need, and in their ability to participate freely in everyday social life, as whole selves. Most poignantly, however, the notion of exile implies that members of such a group will find themselves dispossessed of the language they need in order to formulate and communicate their predicament. They are psychically isolated as well as socially disempowered.

The theme of exile alerts us to some important aspects of Marx's theory of alienation, aspects not often discussed. Alienation means more than the brute exploitation of the workers, certainly more than dissatisfaction with one's work. Alienation is a disaster to the self and the species because, according to Marx, part of what makes us human is being caught up in a web of intrinsic relations to the world and to each other. Because of alienation, the strands of this web are severed.

Alienation is not the opposite of property, therefore, or of power, at least in its sense as "domination." Rather, alienation is the opposite of dialogue. It derails the dialectic of human need so that we tragically pursue what will injure us, so that we choose death instead of life. The model of exile illuminates these most tragic traits of alienation. The model of return suggests that revolution, Marx's remedy for alienation, works to restore the unimpeded exchange between human beings and the world, from which their needs and powers spring: not an end to history, but a renewal.

In capitalist society, all human beings live in exile, but the working class suffers from it most. As a class, however, they do in theory have the power to rise up and remedy their condition. Karl Marx, too, seems to suffer exile as his personal fate. Yet until now, he has apparently been powerless to achieve his repatriation.

We have found that reading Marx through the prism of the Jewish tradition makes us aware of certain underlying dynamics in his work, patterns and problems which crop up again and again. Marx alludes to this texturing of his thought, but he never reflects on it: that is left for us, his readers.

But consider what kind of reader Karl Marx needs. He requires us to be familiar with the Western tradition of political thought. His theory could not exist without the writings of the philosophical canon: he constructs his whole project of research and exposition in reference to them.

Much of what Marx has to say, however, he conveys by how he diverges from previous writers, either explicitly or implicitly. To understand Marx, it is not enough to read his statements about this topic or that. It is not even enough to compare them side by side with the propositions that other thinkers have put forth. We have to measure the specific difference which determines what Marx means to us, not by what he says, but what he does: the transformation he performs on the text he reads.

The reader Marx requires, then, must be able to imagine theory as *theorizing*, as a kind of activity or practice. He or she must also be motivated to ask questions about Marx's practice, in the belief that the answers will teach us all something significant, something which bears more than an arbitrary resemblance to what Marx wrote and which addresses the present needs and difficulties of those who are reading him now.

Besides a grounding in Western philosophy and an interest in theoretical practice, Marx's reader would also do well to know something about Jewish thought. It is not impossible that one could trace the trajectory of Marx's revision of Hegel, for example, and work it backward until one came up with approximately the structures of Jewish thought we use to interpret Marx—but is it believable? Generally, we do not think to ask how philosophers depart from the Greco-Christian tradition in political thought, because they do not. Our task instead is to chart their course within the flows and eddies of that tradition.

If readers were familiar with Jewish thinking as well as Western philosophy and were accustomed to responding in both modes to what they read, they might notice something strange going on when they read Marx. They might sense attitudes and argumentative moves that seem familiar from another place. They might even begin to wonder about Marx and his personal Jewish question.

But we have done this kind of noticing and wondering ourselves—at the very beginning of this essay, when we explored Marx's declaration, "I am no Marxist." The playful explanation at which we arrived—that Marx's theory is left to us unfinished and we have the duty to develop it—we can now recognize as a kind of midrash. All through the body of this work, we have been elaborating on that bit of interpretation. We used our initial conception of how Marx writes to make sense of his key theoretical demarches against the Greeks, Bauer, and Hegel. We laid out his ontology to deepen our understanding of the direction he is taking. More than the doctrines he enunciates, we wrestled with the problems he tackles, central among them the struggle to make what is important to him important to his readers.

In short, we have done what we argued Marx requires his readers to do: a midrash on the interference between the Greco-Christian political tradition which Marx addresses and the Jewish tradition which helps construct his message. We established the context which gives the Jewish question about Marx its meaning. In the process, we began to return Marx from exile.

If exile is the name of the social condition which separates Marx from his potential audience, what are the social forces which sustain it? Why is it difficult for us to read Marx as we conclude he needs to be read? It would be presumptuous to try to answer the question fully, here: the topic calls for an investigation all its own. There are two factors, however, that any answer would have to take into account.

The first is the persistence of antisemitism in modern political thought: not virulent Jew hatred, but the genteel and generally quite unconscious assumption that nothing about Jews or Judaism matters. We saw this assumption at work in mainstream interpretations of "On the Jewish Question," and we saw there how it obscured Marx's point. When Marx wrote, of course, this assumption was explicit and only barely detached from its theological moorings. Furthermore, Marx shared many of the anti-Jewish and antisemitic prejudices of his day. In order to develop his critique of "Christian" politics, he had to invent an "everyday Judaism" from which religion was methodologically excluded, and then proceed by negation. Marx himself could not read—would not be capable of reading—his own work in the way we have.

But even in recent times, most commentators have not been prepared to ask the Jewish question about Marx. Possibly, this inability reflects the residual influence of Sunday-school lessons which taught that God broke off the old covenant with the Jews to collect a new Israel through the Christian church. Possibly, however, the theorists' neglect represents their democratic and not their Christian faith. As Jean-Paul Sartre writes:

> The democrat, like the scientist, fails to use the particular case; to him the individual is only an ensemble of universal traits. It follows that his defense of the Jew saves the latter as man and annihilates him as Jew. . . . His defense is to persuade individuals that they exist in an isolated state. "There are no Jews," he says, "there is no Jewish question." This means that he wants to separate the Jew from his religion, from his family, from his ethnic community, in order to plunge him into the democratic crucible whence he will emerge naked and alone, an individual and solitary particle like all the other particles.[4]

Sartre's shrewd observation leads on to the second reason we find it difficult to do midrash on Marx's Jewishness: the definitions of self, knowledge, and freedom which have marked off the modern age and which have set their imprint on liberal notions of democracy. Before modern times, to be in touch with one's true self, one sought to find one's place in a meaningful cosmic order, using one's God-given powers of reason. The intellectuals of the seventeenth-century Enlightenment more or less reversed this conception. They promoted the idea that being in touch with one's self meant drawing back from the world, refusing to search outside oneself for meaning, and observing the physical and social universe in a detached, objective way in order to gain mastery over both.[5]

This deliberate setting of boundaries between the self and the outside world ushered in what we have come to know as the modern age. Certainly, not everyone has accepted completely the idea that a person is a "self-defining subject," as Taylor calls it, even in theory. No one today can entirely escape its influence, either: it is our tacit understanding of what it means to be a person. Thinking of ourselves this way, however, prevents us from understanding any theory which finds a meaning to human life elsewhere than in the impulses of the individual. We have committed ourselves as moderns to the idea that there is not and cannot ever be a meaning which human beings did not wholly create.

The modern view of the person as a self-defining subject insures that when we do run into claims of purposes larger than ourselves, we are most likely to regard them as threats to our freedom. Freedom, in the modern world, consists first and foremost of the rejection of anything vaguely resembling a meaningful order which could impose its demands on us. This defensive stance sets unspoken limits on what in modernity can count as knowledge. Knowledge is of the world, by the knower. It is universally applicable and communicable to all. If the knower's own situation becomes a part of how he or she knows, then in modernity, we regard that knowledge as somehow tainted, biased, irrational.

Against this background, how can modern people be expected to do a midrashic reading of Marx? To interpret Marx as we have done is to place him within a context of meaning which goes on beyond the individual: not a cosmic order, but an intersubjective structure resembling it closely enough to set off alarm bells in the modern mind. If Marx makes sense best in light of a certain tradition, then by modern standards he is not free, and how shall we learn from him about freedom? Furthermore, Marx calls us to pay attention to human need, a product of our evolving sense of what it is to be human. Surely, this call infringes on the right of every subject to define his or her needs autonomously.

On top of all this, our midrash blends Marx's situation with his theory and our own situation with our understanding of Marx. Unless we are familiar with Jewish thought and refuse to be troubled by questions of method besides, chances are we would never arrive at a reading like this one. Are we not reading into

Marx what we want to hear, projecting what we want to see? How can we call the outcome of such an inquiry "knowledge"?

If we can do so, as we have done throughout this essay, the reason is that modernity is beginning to lose its grip on our sense of reality. Possibly, it had never fully triumphed; the modern notions of self, freedom, and knowledge perhaps had always served as disciplinary ideals, never fully achieved in practice.

In any event, two movements, one theoretical and one primarily social, have eroded these landmarks in the twentieth century. The first is the deconstruction of the subject. When Freud traced our patterns of thought and behavior back to their origins in early childhood, and when Nietzsche analyzed the irrational basis of our values and the covert influence of the will to power on our sense of the real, they dug at the foundations of the modern self. It has never fully recovered.

The women's movement, meanwhile, has heightened our cultural awareness of difference, making it clear that being a specific person is not less than being a self-defining subject, but more. The strain of feminism known as identity politics has sought within each person's experience as a White woman, a Black woman, a Jewish woman, or a Christian woman to find authentic ways of understanding the world and acting in it.[6]

Many contemporary observers of politics remain committed to modernity. They take notice of the fading of the modern subject only to deplore it. The story of Karl Marx and the Jewish question, however, comes to teach us that trying to be a subject may prevent us from discovering who we are and what we need. Those who find the decline of modernity encouraging, therefore, must revive Lenin's question: what is to be done? For something must be done. If liberal politics at its best is designed to make subjects free, but not people, not you and me, then we need a new politics, one that aims to overcome our specific alienation and to emancipate us as distinct human beings: in short, to return us from exile.

What is to be done? In the late part of the twentieth century, the need for a new politics resolves itself into the Jewish question of our times. The Jewish question in Marx's day concerned a people unfitted to be free by the demanding tasks that made them a people. The unmet needs which the Jews embodied put the lie to the lofty claims of the state and helped give rise to a new theory of emancipation. The Jewish question of our times asks: How may we all become free, excluding none of us? How may we seek our individual identities, our communal homes, and our transcendent purposes all at the same time (since that is the only way any of them will be achieved)? From this land of exile, how can we return?

We have said that the way a group is exiled within a society differs from the way a society as a whole can be in exile, even though the two are bound up together. In the same manner, if we want to talk about the condition of Blacks, Hispanics, Asian and Native Americans, white women, gay men, and lesbians in our country, we have to use the term "exile" in a different sense than when we are speaking of the Jews, even though the Jewish case may help us recognize the other exiles.

The Jewish people is unique in that its identity is partially defined by a task, the hallowing of the world, set by a practice, dialogue with God. Being committed to this task and guided by this practice is an important part of what Jewish identity has historically meant. Jews find themselves in this existential situation over and over, in different countries and in every generation, because of a tradition which plants the imperatives of Jewish culture in their core sense of self.

There are other groups, however, which also confute modernity by drawing their identities from still vital roots. Black Americans have claimed a connection to an African culture that preexisted their years of slavery and persecution in the United States. Hispanic, Asian, and Native Americans enjoy lively traditions from long before immigration and colonization. Although the idea of being chosen for a task is not part of their cultures, the need to preserve a sense of identity in the face of hostile attitudes and institutions puts these groups in exile.

More controversially, it is sometimes argued that a women's culture, a gay culture, or a lesbian culture exists in this country, in conflict with the worldview and values of the mainstream. These cultures, if we choose to call them by that term, are not rooted in a tradition in the same way as ethnic cultures. They arise from the experience of oppression or from the perspectives women develop doing the "women's work" that has historically been their lot. The notion of women's culture also tends to ignore that different women have different notions of what is womanly; all too often, it means the ways white, Christian women born into the middle class think and interact.[7]

Nevertheless, being female, gay, or lesbian in the United States today means finding oneself in exile. The realities of the lives of the members of each of these groups, as different as they are from one another, are unrecognized in straight male culture and are burdened by institutions designed on the assumption that they do not matter. All these groups are constituted in ways that exclude them from society and set them in conflict with it. They cannot assimilate without losing a great deal of what makes them the selves they are. They are exiles in need of a politics of return.

In order to be able to pursue their own purposes, members of all these groups need to do what the women's movement calls "consciousness raising": to become aware of their common condition. From consciousness raising, they can enter into dialogue with other exiles, searching for bases for a common struggle. The success of this endeavor is unpredictable because each group is exiled differently; each seeks to return to a different home. Keeping that in mind, however, the exiled groups stand a chance of forming workable coalitions to press their claims on the political order.[8] The goal of a politics of return, however, will not be reached merely by acting within liberal politics. Exiled groups must seek to transform politics: to make dialogue over who they are and what they are doing here into the center of political life, as it is the center of their own lives.

And thus, the return from exile of particular groups leads the way to the return from exile of society. For the exile that affects us all in modernity is the loss of meaning in social life. Liberal democracy, in particular, takes pride in excluding any sense of public purpose from political discourse on principle; public purposes and shared meanings are considered too dangerous to individual liberty to be allowed. But the theme of exile points to the dangers of ignoring our tasks, our narratives, our senses of reality, our human needs. Those dangers are coming more to public attention, even as I write.

With the breakdown of the false unity anticommunism bred in

the United States, we can expect to see a return of the repressed in American politics. Judging from early signs, we are about to hear voices crying anew for a better way of life here at home. Whether those voices come from within ourselves or from our neighbors, we will be better able to interpret them if we listen for intimations that people are protesting their exile. If we understand that about ourselves and others, we improve our chance of getting what we need and of finally fulfilling Karl Marx's project of human emancipation, even in ways he did not expect.

Karl Marx's critique of capitalism remains crucial to any movement that seeks a more human society, both in its specifics—many of them apply to "actually existing socialist" societies, too—and in its insistence that we must change the mode of production in order to set ourselves free. What we are now in a position to learn from Marx, over and above his theories, is how far we have been exiled, and how deeply we long to return. His life is our predicament and our legacy.

Notes

Introduction

1. David McLellan, *Karl Marx: His Life and Thought* (New York: Harper & Row, 1973), p. 443.

2. Karl Schurz, cited in ibid., p. 453.

3. Marx to Lassalle (1842) and Marx to Leske, cited in ibid., p. 304. Marx uses "he" and "man" throughout his writings. He does this partially from convention and partially (despite his awareness of the "woman question") because his theory takes the male experience as the norm. I am leaving Marx's sexist language in place. I encourage readers, however, to ask, each time Marx says "he," whether he intends to include women and whether he succeeds.

4. Paul Ricoeur has defined hermeneutics as "the theory of the operations of understanding in their relation to the interpretation of texts" (*Hermeneutics and the Human Sciences*, ed. John B. Thompson [Cambridge: Cambridge University Press, 1981]). For the hermeneutic circle, see Hans Georg Gadamer, *Philosophical Hermeneutics* (Berkeley: University of California Press, 1977).

5. See J. L. Austin, *How to Do Things with Words*, 2d ed. (Cambridge: Harvard University Press, 1975).

6. Louis Dupré, *Marx's Critique of Culture* (New Haven: Yale University Press, 1983), p. 13. As the last phrase of the quotation implies, however, Dupré maintains a sharper distinction between hermeneutics and critique than the one on which I rely.

7. Sometimes, we do not learn even what he teaches us explicitly. See chapter 4 below.

8. The notion of "essentially contested concepts" comes from W. B. Gallie's essay of the same name in *Proceedings of the Aristotelian Society*, volume 56 (London, 1955–56). For a discussion of essentially contested concepts in political theory, see William E. Connolly, *The Terms of Political Discourse*, 2d ed. (Princeton: Princeton University Press, 1983), chapter 2.

9. Karl Marx, "Theses on Feuerbach," in *The Marx-Engels Reader*, Robert C. Tucker, ed., 2d ed. (New York: W. W. Norton & Company, 1978), p. 143.

10. Saul K. Padover, *Karl Marx: An Intimate Biography* (New York: McGraw-Hill, 1978), pp. 17, 169.

11. McLellan, *Karl Marx*, pp. 2, 86, 6. It is characteristic of the literature that it presumes Marx's relations to Judaism must either be dissolved in the mainstream of the Western tradition or else be conceived as a reduction of theory to religion. The poverty of these alternatives pleads the case for a third approach.

12. Shlomo Avineri, *The Social and Political Thought of Karl Marx* (Cambridge: Cambridge University Press, 1968), p. 4. The term "Judeo-Christian" presumes too much: at various points, this essay throws into relief the vast differences between Judaism and Christianity, as theologies and as ontologies.

13. I am skipping over the treatment by Istvan Meszaros in *Marx's Theory of Alienation* (London: Merlin Press, 1970) because it crudely intermingles Jewish and Christian thought patterns and throws about biblical quotations without ever considering how they are most fruitfully to be read. This textual carelessness stands in contrast to the author's exacting reading of Marx.

14. Julius Carlebach, *Karl Marx and the Radical Critique of Judaism* (London: Routledge & Kegan Paul, 1978), p. 320. But cf. pp. 310–11.

15. Susan Handelman, *The Slayers of Moses* (Albany: State University of New York Press, 1982), p. xv.

16. Bertell Ollman, *Alienation*, 2d ed. (Cambridge: Cambridge University Press, 1976).

17. The will to innovate—to do what the tradition does, even when differing from what it says—is found most strongly in the Reconstructionist and Havurah movements in Judaism today, but it remains a heritage that all Jews can claim.

18. Jerrold Seigel, *Marx's Fate* (Princeton: Princeton University Press, 1978), p. 3.

Chapter 1. Four Jewish Questions about Marx

1. McLellan, *Karl Marx*, p. 80. Of course, liberalism is a particularly porous tradition. To speak of "liberal politics" or "the liberal notion of freedom" is to employ a kind of philosophical shorthand. According to Marx's early writings, modern politics is marked by the centrifugal separation of the state and civil society (see section 3 of this chapter). Liberalism aims at achieving the minimum of coercion by the state but, according to Marx, ignores other, real constraints arising out of civil society. Freedom understood as formal, political freedom is the liberal ideal.

2. Dupré, p. 25.

3. Karl Marx, "On the Jewish Question," in *Marx-Engels Reader*, p. 27.

4. Ibid., pp. 48, 49. Interestingly, in light of our discussion of the Jewish question later in this chapter, the word *Fahigkeit* which translates here as "capacity" can also imply "fittingness" as in *Salonsfahig*, "fit for the salon," that is, polite society.

5. This is contrary to Dagobert D. Runes, who saw fit to publish "On the Jewish Question" as *A World Without Jews* (New York: Philosophical Library, 1959).

6. "On the Jewish Question," in *Marx-Engels Reader*, p. 48.

7. Ibid., pp. 49–50. These are only the particular indictments of Judaism most integral to Marx's argument. The essay also contains offhand accusations such as that Judaism exudes "contempt for theory, for art, for history, and for man as an end in himself" (ibid., p. 51).

8. McLellan, *Karl Marx*, p. 86.

9. Carlebach, pp. 310–11.

10. See the genealogical table in McLellan, *Karl Marx*, p. 466.

11. The reference, p. 7, seems all the more pointed since it echoes the traditional formula of Jewish prayer, "God of Abraham, Isaac, and Jacob."

12. Seigel, pp. 42–43.

13. Carlebach, p. 32.

14. McLellan, *Karl Marx*, p. 5.

15. Padover, p. 48.

16. Seigel, p. 47.

17. McLellan, *Karl Marx*, pp. 9–10; Padover, p. 33.

18. Dupré, p. 67; Padover, pp. 76–77. The *Wissenschaft* movement aimed at refounding Jewish identity on the basis of the scientific study of Jewish history, rather than faith.

19. The term is from Isaac Deutscher, *The Non-Jewish Jew and Other Essays*, ed. Tamara Deutscher (London: Oxford Univ. Press, 1968).

20. McLellan, *Karl Marx*, p. 53.

21. Padover, p. 48.

22. Seigel, p. 89.

23. "On the Jewish Question," p. 26.

24. Cited in ibid., p. 29. (For a full translation of Bauer's article, see *Philosophical Forum* 2–4 [1978]: 135–49.) Emphasis in original.

25. "On the Jewish Question," p. 31.

26. Ibid., p. 33.

27. McLellan, *Karl Marx*, p. 37.

28. "On the Jewish Question," p. 30.

29. Ibid., p. 40.

30. Ibid., p. 46.

31. Karl Marx, "Contribution to the Critique of Hegel's *Philosophy of Right,*" in *Marx-Engels Reader,* p. 21.

32. Ibid., pp. 32–33.

33. "On the Jewish Question," p. 46.

34. For a fuller discussion of Marx's theory of human needs, see chapter 3 below.

35. "On the Jewish Question," pp. 45, 43.

36. Ibid., p. 46.

37. Joel Schwartz actually does note this contrast, but by treating "Judaism" as synonymous with "Sabbath Judaism," he misses the point. See "Liberalism and the Jewish Connection," *Political Theory,* Feb. 1985, pp. 58–84.

38. "On the Jewish Question," pp. 36, 38, 52. Perhaps this explains the comment of Marx's Cologne acquaintance with Georg Jung, "For Marx, at any rate, the Christian religion is one of the most immoral there is" (McLellan, *Karl Marx,* p. 42).

39. "On the Jewish Question," p. 48 (for a thorough examination of Marx's views on "Sabbath Judaism," see Schwartz).

40. "On the Jewish Question," pp. 48, 50, 51, 52.

41. Ibid., p. 48.

42. McLellan, *Karl Marx,* p. 457.

43. "Theses on Feuerbach," p. 143.

44. I am not concerned here with the vexed question of how symbols function generally, but rather with how they work in Marx's thinking. The theme "Judaism" seems to form a link in a chain that binds human needs with civil society and both with a practical and realistic refusal of the claims of the political state. Moreover, I argue, these elements are related internally, so that Marx moves from one to the next effortlessly, by process of association. To use the terminology of literary theory, symbols in Marx's thought function as metonymies rather than as metaphors. See Handelman, pp. 54–55.

45. Seigel, pp. 117–18.

46. See Jacob R. Marcus, *The Jew in the Medieval World: A Source Book* (Cincinnati: Union of American Hebrew Congregations, 1938), pp. 41–42, 145, and *Judaism on Trial,* ed. Hyam Maccoby, (Rutherford, N.J.: Fairleigh Dickinson University Press, 1982).

47. Carlebach, pp. 12–17.

48. Hans Liebeschutz, "German Radicalism and the Formation of Jewish Political Attitudes during the Early Part of the Nineteenth Century," in *Studies in Nineteenth Century Jewish Intellectual History,* ed. Alexander Altmann (Cambridge: Harvard University Press, 1964), p. 145.

49. Carlebach, pp. 23–24.

50. Liebeschutz, p. 142.

51. Jacob Katz, "The Term 'Jewish Emancipation': Its Origins and Historical Impact," in Altmann, pp. 9–10.

52. Ibid., p. 21.

53. Jews tended to respond by challenging the credentials of Christian Europe to pass judgment on questions of freedom. Heinrich Heine, Marx's contemporary, asked rhetorically, "What is the greatest assignation of our times? It is the emancipation, not only of the people of Ireland, of the Greeks, the Jews of Frankfurt, the blacks of West India and similar depressed peoples, but of the whole world, especially Europe" (ibid.). Ludwig Bornes, a slightly older reformer, added: "Seen from the European point of view, Germany as a whole was a ghetto" (Liebeschutz, p. 14).

54. Leon Poliakov, "Anti-Semitism and Christian Teaching," *Midstream* 12 (March 1966): 13. Cited in John Murray Cuddihy, *The Ordeal of Civility* (New York: Basic Books, 1974), pp. ix, 4.

55. Ibid., pp. 14, 68. *Halakha* actually translates better as "way of going" although it can also include "law."

56. See Schwartz, p. 82, n. 64. See also chapter 4 below.

57. Nathan Rotenstreich, *Jews and German Philosophy* (New York: Schocken Books, 1984), p. 81.

58. Ludwig Feuerbach, *The Essence of Christianity*, trans. George Eliot (New York: Harper & Brothers, 1957), p. 114.

59. Marx W. Wartofsky, *Feuerbach* (Cambridge: Cambridge University Press, 1977), p. 321.

60. Carlebach, pp. 10–11, 372.

61. "On the Jewish Question," p. 52.

62. Seigel, pp. 144–45.

63. "On the Jewish Question," p. 48.

64. Seigel notes this tendency in the contrasting analyses of the 1848 revolution Marx gives in *The Class Struggle in France* and *The Eighteenth Brumaire of Louis Bonaparte* (pp. 199–203).

Chapter 2. The Power of the Tongue

1. Jacques Derrida, *Writing and Difference*, trans. Alan Bass (Chicago: University of Chicago Press, 1978), p. 118. The novelist to whom he refers is James Joyce.

2. Ibid., p. 82.

3. In this light, speaking of Marx's ontology (as I do in the title of chapter 3) can only mean posing the question of how the way Marx understands reality is or is not like what Western thought refers to as *ontology*, without prejudging the issue.

4. Robert Alter, *The Art of Biblical Narrative* (New York: Basic Books, 1981), p. 32n.

5. Karl Marx, "Introduction to the *Critique of Hegel's Philosophy of*

Right," in *Karl Marx: Early Writings,* trans. T. B. Bottomore (New York: McGraw-Hill, 1963), p. 52.

6. The Babylonian Talmud is a written record of the oral tradition of commentary on the Bible that had developed by the year 200 c.e. It also includes later rabbinic glosses. See chapter 4 below.

7. Matthew Arnold, *Culture and Anarchy* (New York: Macmillan, 1896), p. 109, cited in Handelman, p. 179.

8. Johannes Pedersen, *Israel: Its Life and Culture,* trans. Mrs. Aslaug Moller (London: Oxford University Press, 1926—47).

9. Thorleif Boman, *Hebrew Thought Compared with Greek* (New York: W. W. Norton, 1960), pp. 189, 27.

10. Ibid., pp. 54, 119—21, 86.

11. Ibid., pp. 128, 184.

12. Aristotle, *Ethica Nicomathea,* 1177a—1179a. See also Hannah Arendt, *The Human Condition* (Chicago: University of Chicago Press, 1958).

13. Martha C. Nussbaum, *The Fragility of Goodness* (Cambridge: Cambridge University Press, 1986).

14. See Nussbaum's discussion of the different translations of *phainomena,* pp. 240—45.

15. Dante represents this attitude when he proves the earth does not move by citing Aristotle, "that glorious philosopher to whom above all others Nature disclosed her secrets." See Henry Osborn Taylor, *The Classical Heritage of the Middle Ages* (New York: Frederick Ungar Publishing Co., 1957), p. 46n.

16. Boman, p. 31.

17. Ibid., p. 38.

18. Ibid., p. 150.

19. Ibid., pp. 146, 126—27.

20. Ibid., pp. 137, 140.

21. Ibid., p. 148.

22. Yosef Hayim Yerushalmi, *Zakhor: Jewish History and Jewish Memory* (Seattle: University of Washington Press, 1982), p. 44.

23. Ibid., p. 171. Note that eschatology does not imply a *telos* since we can still argue with God over our final ends. Also, readers familiar with Martin Heidegger's *Being and Time* will note some similarity between his view of time and history and the biblical view I have been presenting. Cf. Michael Wyschogrod, *The Body of Faith* (New York: Seabury Press, 1983).

24. Boman, pp. 156—57.

25. Ibid., p. 159.

26. Ibid., p. 160.

27. Ibid., pp. 185, 117, 91.

28. Goethe, *Faust,* cited ibid., p. 191n.

29. Ibid., p. 65.

30. Boman fails to examine either language "as a whole," uses terms like *static* and *dynamic* absolutely instead of along a continuum with other languages, and makes his comparisons along dimensions that would produce nonsensical results if applied to ancient Egyptian or modern German, for example. James Barr, *The Semantics of Biblical Language* (Glasgow: Oxford University Press, 1961), p. 21.

31. "Boman's habit of contrasting Hebrew language with its alleged implications with Greek thought and not in the first place with Greek linguistic structure" only obscures the issue further. Ibid., p. 75.

32. Ibid., p. 69.

33. To use language at all, people must structure their utterances according to "linguistic form and type," which may have nothing to do with "distinctions in the actual objects." Grammatical gender, for instance—the rules by which various languages determine at what points to assign a gender to objects, or to maintain a correspondence between gender and sex—"is a prime example of a linguistic structure which cannot be taken to reflect a thought problem." Ibid., p. 40.

34. Ibid., pp. 25–26. Barr contradicts the influential Sapir-Whorf hypothesis, which tells us, "Human beings . . . are very much at the mercy of the particular language which has become the medium for their society." Edmund Sapir, *Selected Writings,* cited in Amy Tan, "The Language of Discretion," in *The State of the Language,* ed. Christopher Ricks and Leonard Michaels (Berkeley: University of California Press, 1990), pp. 25–32.

35. Scholars grouped under the rubric of biblical theology make much of the fact that Christianity "belongs with Jewish thought as a roughly homogeneous entity clearly set apart from the other currents of European thought" (Barr, pp. 8–9). This preconceived notion heightens the reader's awareness of any linguistic feature which seems to make Hebrew thought more idiosyncratic, at the same time classifying evidence which does not bear on the issue as neutral (ibid., p. 23). I have picked out and summarized only those of Barr's criticisms I think one must evaluate before adopting a Hebrew-Greek distinction.

36. See note 28. One apparent exception is Boman's treatment of the Greek and Hebrew word for *word.* He calls the term a "point of intersection" between the two modes and reads "the Word" of the Gospel of John as effecting "a beautiful and mysterious unity" of Greek and Hebrew (pp. 68–69). Yet even here, Boman stresses that the resemblance is purely formal: "These two terms teach us what the two peoples considered primary and essential in mental life."

37. Lewis Carroll, *Through the Looking-Glass,* in *The Annotated Alice,* ed. Martin Gardner (New York: Bramhall House, 1960), p. 207.

38. But see Humpty Dumpty's explanation, ibid., pp. 269–70.

39. Handelman, p. 37.

40. Barry W. Holtz, "On Reading Jewish Texts," in *Back to the Sources*, ed. Barry W. Holtz (New York: Summit Books, 1984), p. 29.

41. This holds true even for Jewish secularists, including those who base their identities on the history of the Jews as an outsider people. See Lawrence Bush, "The Bundist's Sabbath," *Genesis 2* (April/May 1986): 16–19. Nevertheless, even though certain themes in the Torah are basic to Jewish culture, not all Jews accept them or are aware of them; nor do these themes exhaust the resources of Jewish thought.

42. Joel Rosenberg, "Biblical Narrative," in Holtz, p. 31.

43. Bruce Kawin, *Telling It Again and Again*, cited in Alter, p. 92.

44. It would be possible to investigate what view of reality other genres represented in the Torah express, too, and to compare law with poetry, or narrative with prayer. For our purpose, the biblical narrative is a close enough approximation of the whole text.

45. Rosenberg, pp. 62–63.

46. Alter, p. 65.

47. Ibid., p. 182.

48. Martin Buber, *The Origin and Meaning of Hasidism*, trans. Maurice Friedman (New York: Harper & Row, 1960), p. 31.

49. Alter, p. 12.

50. Sifre Numbers 112, cited in Handelman, p. 70.

51. Boman, p. 49.

52. Aristotle, *Ethica Nicomathea*, 1155a–1157a, 1166a–b, 1169b–1170b.

53. Alter, pp. 126–27.

54. Buber, *Origin and Meaning*, p. 94.

55. Rosenberg, p. 47.

Chapter 3. Greek and Hebrew in Marx's Ontology

1. Charles Taylor, *Hegel* (Cambridge: Cambridge University Press, 1975), p. 25.

2. Ibid., p. 26.

3. Marx applies this label to Hegel on the opening page of his doctoral dissertation, "The Difference between the Democritean and the Epicurean Philosophy of Nature," translated in Norman Livergood, *Activity in Marx's Philosophy* (The Hague: Martinus Nijhoff, 1967), pp. 61–109.

4. Taylor, *Hegel*, p. 172.

5. Ibid., pp. 172–76, 377–78.

6. Cited in Seigel, p. 66.

7. Ibid., p. 67.

8. Livergood, pp. 71–72.

9. Ibid., p. 69.

10. Ibid., p. 70.

11. Karl to Heinrich Marx (1837), quoted in McLellan, *Karl Marx*, p. 28.

12. Avineri, p. 18.

13. Seigel, pp. 106, 134.

14. Ibid., p. 106.

15. See ibid., pp. 175–76, and compare Karl Marx and Friedrich Engels, *Manifesto of the Communist Party*, in *Marx-Engels Reader*, pp. 493–96. In the *Grundrisse*, Marx writes on Greek art in a more detached manner, indicating a shift in symbology but not a change in theme.

16. Even if we happen to disagree with Marx's critique of "Greece," and even if it does not exactly parallel the account of Greek thought we gave in chapter 2, we can still recognize the central part it plays in the evolution of his theory.

17. On Moses, see Carlebach, p. 317, and Marx, "Introduction to the *Critique of Hegel's Philosophy of Right*," p. 45. On Joshua, see Avineri, p. 43. On Levites, see *The Grundrisse*, ed. David McLellan (New York: Harper & Row, 1971), p. 20. On Adam, see *Grundrisse*, trans. Martin Nicolaus (New York: Random House, 1973), p. 611. On Esau, see ibid., p. 307. On Habakkuk, see "The Eighteenth Brumaire of Louis Bonaparte," in *Marx-Engels Reader*, p. 596. On Ezekiel, see ibid., p. 614. The list is not comprehensive.

18. "Old Testament" is a derogatory title given to the Hebrew Bible by the early Christians. "Testament" means "covenant," and the name *Old Testament* refers to the doctrine that God abrogated the original covenant with the Jews in order to replace them with the Christians as a chosen people. In this essay, we will use the term *Torah* instead.

19. Marx to Lassalle, cited in *Grundrisse* (1973), pp. 59–60.

20. Ollman, p. 17.

21. This elasticity of meaning is what Ollman intends when he paraphrases Pareto, saying, "Marx's words are like bats: one can see in them both birds and mice" (p. 3). Marx can do this with his words, according to Ollman, because the different meanings of the same concept are internally related in his theory. Marx's use of context to establish meaning resembles the biblical use of key-words that we discussed in the previous chapter and some kinds of rabbinic word-play to be mentioned in chapter 4. Ibid., p. 15.

22. *1844 Manuscripts*, in *Early Writings*, p. 207.

23. Ollman, pp. 89, 92.

24. Marx accuses Max Stirner, Jeremy Bentham, and the German

"true socialists" of ideological thinking, each in the defense of a different interest. Ibid., pp. xii–xiii, 227–32, 292n.

25. Ibid., pp. 82–83.

26. See Ollman's discussion of why Marx calls the alienated individual an "abstraction," pp. 134–35.

27. Carol Gould, *Marx's Social Ontology* (Cambridge: MIT Press, 1978), p. xvi.

28. *1844 Manuscripts*, p. 207.

29. Karl Marx, "Preface to the *Critique of Political Economy*," in *Marx-Engels Reader*, pp. 4–5.

30. "To talk about the realization of a self here is to say that the adequate human life would not be just a fulfillment of an idea or a plan which is fixed independently of the subject who realizes it, as in the Aristotelian form of a man. Rather, this life must have the added dimension that the subject can recognize it as his own, as having unfolded from within him. This self-related dimension is entirely missing from the Aristotelian tradition." Taylor, *Hegel*, p. 15. Marx adds that this life does not merely unfold: we create it through productive practice.

31. Ollman, pp. 114–19.

32. See William E. Connolly, *Appearance and Reality in Politics* (Cambridge: Cambridge University Press, 1981), pp. 173–74.

33. Taylor, *Hegel*, pp. 557–58.

34. Karl Marx, *Capital*, vol. 3, trans. Samuel Moore and Edward Aveling (New York: International Publishers, 1967), pp. 818–20.

35. See Friedrich Nietzsche, *The Will to Power*, trans. Walter Kaufman and R. J. Hollingsdale (New York: Vintage, 1967), p. 17.

36. Marx, "On the Jewish Question," p. 51.

37. Taylor, *Hegel*, p. 557.

38. See note 14.

39. "Rabbi" is a Hebrew term meaning "my teacher." Rabbis are not clergy in the Christian sense. They do not act as intercessors between their congregants and God, nor do they have to have a calling in order to serve (although good character is presumed). Rather, the rabbinic movement, beginning in the first century c.e., based its claim to authority on scholarship: in particular, on the ability to find new, powerful interpretations of the Torah which would help organize Jewish life and thought. For an account of the remarkable way the rabbinic movement transformed Judaism, see Jacob Neusner, *Midrash in Context* (Philadelphia: Fortress Press, 1983).

Chapter 4. Reading and Writing Marx

1. Marx, *Capital*, 1:18–20 (afterword to the second German edition).

2. Avineri, p. 250.

3. At least, Jews have interpreted the argument this way. Living in Christian societies, Jews are repeatedly asked, "Why don't you believe in Christ?" Jews respond that the world after Jesus is just as violent, unjust, and immoral as it was before: Jesus did not live up to the role of the Messiah as outlined in Jewish tradition. But this may not be how Christians see the problem at all. "For Christians, there is no 'world' in the sense of a totality. (Some) *humans* are redeemed, or can be—but here Calvinists differ from Catholics from Lutherans, etc." (Shane Phelan, personal communication).

4. Joan Cocks, "Hegel's Logic, Marx's Science, Rationalism's Perils," *Political Studies* 31 (1983): 592.

5. See Tucker on Marx's use of "transformational criticism" Feuerbach-style in *The Marx-Engels Reader,* introduction, pp. xxii–xxiv.

6. See note 3 to the introduction.

7. Taylor, *Hegel,* p. 327. Emphasis added.

8. The proletariat, according to Marx in 1843, can legitimately consider itself a universal class "because its sufferings are universal": it needs to be liberated from every form of oppression and dehumanization known to history ("Contribution to the Critique of Hegel's *Philosophy of Right:* Introduction," p. 64). This utopian formulation expresses Marx's disgust with the intellectual narrowness of German politics, which he believed would never produce human emancipation out of anything but dire necessity. France, on the other hand, was proceeding from political to human emancipation at least partly on the basis of its *idea* of liberty. Note the cultural basis of movements for emancipation in Marx's early theory.

In *Capital,* Marx drops the theme of the universal class. There, he says the workers will revolt because of the breakdown of the capitalist system, which they will not need a privileged standpoint to see.

9. Robert Paul Wolff traces the ironic structure of *Capital* beautifully in *Moneybags Must Be So Lucky: On the Literary Structure of Marx's "Capital"* (Amherst: University of Massachusetts Press, 1988).

10. See Geoffrey H. Hartman and Sanford Budick, eds., *Midrash and Literature* (New Haven: Yale University Press, 1986); Harold Bloom, *Kabbalah and Criticism* (New York: Seabury Press, 1975); and Jacques Derrida, "Edmond Jabes and the Question of the Book," in *Writing and Difference.*

11. See Arthur Waskow, *Godwrestling* (New York: Schocken Books, 1978).

12. Bereishit Rabbah 1:1, cited in Handelman, p. 67.

13. Jerusalem Talmud Shekalim 13b, cited in Handelman, p. 37. See also Rashi's commentary on Deuteronomy 33:2.

14. Babylonian Talmud Avot 5:21, cited in Handelman, p. 27.

15. Bereishit Rabbah 22:2, cited in Handelman, p. 51.

16. Women were "excused" from the study of the Torah on the grounds that it might conflict with their household duties. Several women became learned anyway, notably Ima Shalom in the third century and the daughters of Rashi, the famous exegete, in the thirteenth century. Today, even the most Orthodox recognize the scholarship of Nechama Leibowitz. Blu Greenberg, the author of *On Women and Judaism: A View from Tradition* (Philadelphia: Jewish Publication Society, 1981) has predicted that we will see the first Orthodox women rabbis before the year 2000. This is a logical but much belated corollary of the attitude toward the Torah described in this chapter.

17. Some of the early Christian church fathers evidently took this approach for many of the stated reasons. See Karlfried Froehlich, *Biblical Interpretation in the Early Church* (Philadelphia: Fortress Press, 1984).

18. "Just as the hammer splits the rock into many fragments, so may one verse be split into many meanings," Babylonian Talmud Sanhedrin, 34a.

19. Babylonian Talmud Avot 1:1.

20. Neusner, *Midrash in Context.*

21. Thus Christian authorities continuously attacked the Talmud as a tissue of lies and slanders, and sometimes succeeded in banning it altogether, along with (in one case) the midrashic mode of sermonizing within the synagogue. See Yvonne Glickson, "Talmud, Burning of," *Encyclopedia Judaica* 15: 768–71.

22. Joseph Dan, "Midrash and the Dawn of Kabbalah," in Hartman and Budick, p. 127.

23. Jerusalem Talmud Peah 17:1, cited in Yerushalmi, p. 112.

24. Babylonian Talmud Shabbat 63a, cited in Handelman, p. 55.

25. Max Kadushin, *The Rabbinic Mind,* 2d ed. (New York: Blaisdell Publishing Co., 1965).

26. Ibid., p. 78.

27. Ibid., p. 134.

28. The concept of "bracketing" comes from the phenomenology of Edmund Husserl. See vol. 3 of his *Collected Works,* trans. Richard Rojcewicz and Andre Schuwer (Dordrecht, The Netherlands: Kluwer Academic Publishers, 1989), p. 27.

29. Kadushin, p. 133. See also Martin Buber, *Two Types of Faith* (New York: Macmillan, 1951).

30. James Kugel, "Two Introductions to Midrash," *Prooftexts* 3 (1983): 131–34.

31. Babylonian Talmud Pesahim 6b, cited in Handelman, p. 37.

32. Kadushin, p. 135.

33. For a discussion of midrash as a literary form rather than an activity, see Addison G. Wright, "The Literary Genre Midrash," *Catholic Biblical Quarterly* 28 (1966): 105–38, 417–57.

34. Louis Althusser and Etienne Balibar, *Reading Capital*, trans. Ben Brewster (London: Verso, 1970), p. 18.

35. Marx, *Capital*, 1:19–20. We might wonder why Marx has an attack by Mendelssohn, an assimilated Jew, on Spinoza, a Jewish heretic, on his mind at this time.

36. See Handelman, pp. 51–76, for a comparison of the logic of midrash halakhah with the logic of Aristotle.

37. Marx, "Contribution to the Critique," p. 18.

38. Ibid., pp. 20–21. Note that Marx draws a relation between form and content which parallels his way of talking about the general and the particular, and which fits easily with the distinctions Boman finds in Hebrew thought (see chapter 2).

39. Althusser does not analyze Marx's use of Hegel because he contends that Marx never was a Hegelian of any sort (*Reading Capital*, pp. 50–51). Although this position seems to disregard Marx's "confession" to his father that he had adopted Hegel over Kant ("Discovering Hegel," in *Marx-Engels Reader*, pp. 7–8), Althusser has a point. If we accept the account given in this chapter and chapter 3, what Marx finds meaningful in Hegel is his critical perspective on Greek thought. He wants to use Hegel to get outside Western philosophy but is disappointed in his hope. That is entirely different from once believing what Hegel did and then changing his mind.

40. Althusser and Balibar, p. 17.

41. For other, varied criticisms of Althusser's approach, see Connolly, *Appearance and Reality in Politics*, pp. 41–62; John O'Neill, *For Marx Against Althusser* (Washington, D.C.: University Press of America, 1982), pp. 1–17; Steven B. Smith, *Reading Althusser* (Ithaca, N.Y.: Cornell University Press, 1984); and E. P. Thompson, *The Poverty of Theory* (London: Merlin Press, 1978).

42. Handelman, pp. 137–40, 174–78.

43. Marx, *Capital* 1:19 (afterword to the second German edition).

Chapter 5. Alienation as Exile

1. See the discussion in Meszaros, pp. 217–27, and also the list of references in Ollman, p. 304, n. 1 on chapter 24.

2. See note 56 on chapter 1 above.

3. See, for example, Kenneth Keniston, *Young Radicals* (New York: Harcourt, Brace, & World, 1968).

4. See G. A. Cohen, *Karl Marx's Theory of History: A Defence* (Princeton: Princeton University Press, 1978).

5. See Erich Fromm's introduction to the 1844 manuscripts in *Marx's Concept of Man* (New York: n.p., 1963).

6. Alasdair C. MacIntyre, *After Virtue* (Notre Dame, Ind.: University of Notre Dame Press, 1981), p. 206.

7. Ibid., p. 210.

8. See our earlier discussion of *hayah* in chapter 2 above. *Hayta* is the feminine perfect form of the verb in biblical Hebrew.

9. This is a paraphrase of a general sketch of Luria's complex doctrine. It is described in more detail in Gershom G. Scholem, *Major Trends in Jewish Mysticism* (New York: Schocken Books, 1954), pp. 260–78.

10. Although the themes of dialogue, exile, and return are centuries-old in Judaism, they have been rejuvenated only in the twentieth century, in very different ways, by Gershom Scholem and Martin Buber. Within Jewish circles, two tendencies oppose this trend. Certain Orthodox thinkers champion the continuing sufficiency of halakhah as the center of Jewish life, setting questions of ultimate meaning to one side. Many less traditional Jews, on the other hand, do not accept exile as a problem because of their faith in rationalism.

11. Unlike Michael Walzer, *Exodus and Revolution* (New York: Basic Books, 1985), I do not focus on the story of the going out of Egypt. The process through which the Jews were enslaved is not a story of exile but a lesson in what happens when a holy people tries to play power politics (see Waskow, *Godwrestling*). Marx's model of revolution is more like returning from exile than leaving Egypt, especially Walzer's antiradical reading of Exodus, skillful as it is.

12. Bereishit Rabbah 3:1.

13. Martin Buber, *On the Bible,* ed. Nahum N. Glatzer (New York: Schocken Books, 1982), p. 18.

14. Waskow, pp. 47–48.

15. Harold Bloom, *Agon: Toward a Theory of Revisionism* (New York: Oxford University Press, 1982), p. 321.

16. See Jacob Katz, *Exclusiveness and Tolerance* (New York: Schocken Books, 1961).

17. *1844 Manuscripts*, pp. 124–25.

18. *Capital* 1: 231–302.

19. *1844 Manuscripts*, pp. 121–29.

20. The idea that maintaining one's identity and worldview are interests of equal importance to the economic ones is expounded in Karl Mannheim, *Ideology and Utopia,* trans. Louis Wirth and Edward Shils (New York; Harcourt, Brace & Co., 1936).

21. Cited in Ollman, p. 304n.

22. Ibid., p. 156.

23. See Marx's discussion of the "fetishism of commodities" in *Capital* 1: 71–83.

24. See Ollman, pp. 174–86.

25. Seigel discusses the theme of the inverted world in Hegel and Marx, pp. 32–37.

Conclusion. Political Discourse in Exile

1. Martin Buber, *Tales of the Hasidim: The Later Masters*, trans. Olga Marx (New York: Schocken Books, 1948), p. 89.

2. Cited in Ollman, p. 35.

3. *Grundrisse* (1973), pp. 61–62.

4. Jean-Paul Sartre, *Anti-Semite and Jew*, trans. George J. Becker (New York: Schocken Books, 1948), pp. 56–57. I do not endorse Sartre's broader theory of anti-Semitism, however.

5. Taylor, *Hegel*, pp. 3–11.

6. See Combahee River Collective, "A Black Feminist Statement," in *This Bridge Called My Back*, ed. Cherrie Moraga and Gloria Anzaldua, 2d ed. (New York: Kitchen Table Press, 1983), pp. 210–18. See also Elly Bulkin, Barbara Smith, and Minnie Bruce Pratt, *Yours in Struggle* (New York: Long Haul Press, 1984). For critical views of identity politics, see Shane Phelan, *Identity Politics* (Philadelphia: Temple University Press, 1989) and Jenny Bourne, "Homelands of the Mind," *Race and Class* 29, no. 1 (1987): 1–23.

7. See Elizabeth V. Spelman, *Inessential Woman* (Boston: Beacon Press, 1988).

8. See Bernice Johnson Reagon, "Coalition Politics: Turning the Century," in *Home Girls*, ed. Barbara Smith (New York: Kitchen Table Press, 1983).

Bibliography

Alter, Robert. *The Art of Biblical Narrative.* New York: Basic Books, 1981.

Althusser, Louis, and Etienne Balibar. *Reading Capital.* Trans. Ben Brewster. London: Verso, 1970.

Altmann, Alexander, ed. *Studies in Nineteenth-Century Jewish Intellectual History.* Cambridge: Harvard University Press, 1964.

Arendt, Hannah. *The Human Condition.* Chicago: University of Chicago Press, 1958.

Aristotle. *Ethica Nicomathea.* Trans. W. D. Ross. Oxford: Clarendon Press, 1925.

Arnold, Matthew. *Culture and Anarchy.* New York: Macmillan, 1896.

Austin, J. L. *How to Do Things with Words.* Ed. J. O. Urmson and Marina Sbisa. 2d ed. Cambridge: Harvard University Press, 1975.

Avineri, Shlomo. *The Social and Political Thought of Karl Marx.* Cambridge: Cambridge University Press, 1968.

Barr, James. *The Semantics of Biblical Language.* Glasgow: Oxford University Press, 1961.

Bauer, Bruno. "The Capacity of Present-Day Jews and Christians to Become Free." Trans. Michael P. Malloy. *Philosophical Forum* 2–4 (1978): 135–49.

Bloom, Harold. *Agon: Toward a Theory of Revisionism.* New York: Oxford University Press, 1982.

———. *Kabbalah and Criticism.* New York: Seabury Press, 1975.

Boman, Thorleif. *Hebrew Thought Compared with Greek.* New York: W. W. Norton and Co., 1960.

Bourne, Jenny. "Homelands of the Mind: Jewish Feminism and Identity Politics." *Race and Class* 29, no. 1 (1987): 1–23.

Bruns, Gerald L. *Inventions: Writing, Textuality, and Understanding in Literary History.* New Haven: Yale University Press, 1982.

Buber, Martin. *On the Bible: Eighteen Studies.* Ed. Nahum N. Glatzer. New York: Schocken Books, 1982.

————. *The Origin and Meaning of Hasidism.* Trans. Maurice Friedman. New York: Harper and Row, 1960.

————. *Tales of the Hasidim.* 2 vols. Trans. Olga Marx. New York: Schocken Books, 1948.

————. *Two Types of Faith.* New York: Macmillan, 1951.

Bulkin, Elly, Barbara Smith, and Minnie Bruce Pratt. *Yours in Struggle: Three Feminist Perspectives on Antisemitism and Racism.* New York: Long Haul Press, 1984.

Bush, Lawrence. "The Bundist's Sabbath." *Genesis 2* (April/May 1986): 16–19.

Carlebach, Julius. *Karl Marx and the Radical Critique of Judaism.* London: Routledge & Kegan Paul, 1978.

Carroll, Lewis. *Through the Looking-Glass and What Alice Found There.* In *The Annotated Alice.* Ed. Martin Gardner. New York: Bramhall House, 1960.

Cocks, Joan. "Hegel's Logic, Marx's Science, Rationalism's Perils." *Political Studies* 31 (1983): 584–603.

Cohen, G. A. *Karl Marx's Theory of History: A Defence.* Princeton: Princeton University Press, 1978.

Combahee River Collective. "A Black Feminist Statement." In *This Bridge Called My Back,* ed. Cherrie Moraga and Gloria Anzaldua, 210–18. New York: Kitchen Table Press, 1983.

Connolly, William E. *Appearance and Reality in Politics.* Cambridge: Cambridge University Press, 1981.

————. *The Terms of Political Discourse.* 2d ed. Princeton: Princeton University Press, 1983.

Cuddihy, John Murray. *The Ordeal of Civility: Freud, Marx, Lévi-Strauss, and the Jewish Struggle with Modernity.* New York: Basic Books, 1974.

Derrida, Jacques. *Writing and Difference.* Trans. Alan Bass. Chicago: University of Chicago Press, 1978.

Deutscher, Isaac. *The Non-Jewish Jew and Other Essays.* Ed. Tamara Deutscher. London: Oxford University Press, 1968.

Dupré, Louis. *Marx's Social Critique of Culture.* New Haven: Yale University Press, 1983.

Feuerbach, Ludwig. *The Essence of Christianity.* Trans. George Eliot. New York: Harper & Brothers, 1957.

Florence, Ronald. *Marx's Daughters.* New York: Dial Press, 1975.

Froehlich, Karlfried. *Biblical Interpretation in the Early Church.* Philadelphia: Fortress Press, 1984.

Fromm, Erich. *Marx's Concept of Man.* New York: n.p., 1963.

Gadamer, Hans Georg. *Philosophical Hermeneutics.* Ed. David E. Linge. Berkeley: University of California Press, 1977.

Gallie, W. B. "Essentially Contested Concepts." *Proceedings of the Aristotelian Society,* vol. 56. London: 1955–56.

Glickson, Yvonne. "Talmud, Burning of." *Encyclopedia Judaica* 15: 768–71.

Gould, Carol C. *Marx's Social Ontology: Individuality and Community in Marx's Theory of Social Reality.* Cambridge: MIT Press, 1978.

Greenberg, Blu. *On Women and Judaism: A View from Tradition.* Philadelphia: Jewish Publication Society, 1981.

Handelman, Susan A. *The Slayers of Moses: The Emergence of Rabbinic Interpretation in Modern Literary Theory.* Albany: State University of New York Press, 1982.

Hartman, Geoffrey H., and Sanford Budick, eds. *Midrash and Literature.* New Haven: Yale University Press, 1986.

Holtz, Barry W., ed. *Back to the Sources: Reading the Classic Jewish Texts.* New York: Summit Books, 1984.

Husserl, Edmund. *Collected Works.* Trans. Richard Rojcewicz and Andre Schuwer. Dordrecht, The Netherlands: Kluwer Academic Publishers, 1989.

Kadushin, Max. *The Rabbinic Mind.* 2d ed. New York: Blaisdell Publishing Company, 1965.

Katz, Jacob. *Exclusiveness and Tolerance.* New York: Schocken Books, 1961.

Keniston, Kenneth. *Young Radicals: Notes on Committed Youth.* New York: Harcourt, Brace & World, 1968.

Kugel, James. "Two Introductions to Midrash." *Prooftexts* 3 (1983): 131–55.

Livergood, Norman D. *Activity in Marx's Philosophy.* The Hague: Martinus Nijhoff, 1967.

Maccoby, Hyam. *Judaism on Trial: Jewish-Christian Disputations in the Middle Ages.* Rutherford, N.J.: Fairleigh Dickinson University Press, 1982.

MacIntyre, Alasdair C. *After Virtue: A Study in Moral Theory.* Notre Dame, Ind.: Notre Dame University Press, 1981.

McLellan, David. *Karl Marx: His Life and Thought.* New York: Harper and Row, 1973.

Mannheim, Karl. *Ideology and Utopia.* Trans. Louis Wirth and Edward Shils. New York: Harcourt, Brace & Co., 1936.

Marcus, Jacob R. *The Jew in the Medieval World: A Source Book.* Cincinnati: Union of American Hebrew Congregations, 1938.

Marx, Karl. *Capital.* 3 vols. Trans. Samuel Moore and Edward Aveling. New York: International Publishers, 1967.

———. *Early Writings.* Trans. T. B. Bottomore. New York: McGraw-Hill, 1963.

———. *The Grundrisse.* ed. David McLellan. New York: Harper and Row, 1971.

———. *Grundrisse: Foundations of the Critique of Political Economy.* Trans. Martin Nicolaus. New York: Random House, 1973.

The Marx-Engels Reader. Ed. Robert C. Tucker. 2d ed. New York: W. W. Norton & Co., 1978.

Marx, Karl, and Friedrich Engels. *The German Ideology.* Ed. C. J. Arthur. New York: International Publishers, 1970.

Meszaros, Istvan. *Marx's Theory of Alienation.* London: Merlin Press, 1970.

Neusner, Jacob. *Midrash in Context.* Philadelphia: Fortress Press, 1983.

Nietzsche, Friedrich. *The Will to Power.* Trans. Walter Kaufman and R. J. Hollingsdale. New York: Vintage, 1967.

Nussbaum, Martha C. *The Fragility of Goodness: Luck and Ethics in Greek Tragedy and Philosophy.* Cambridge: Cambridge University Press, 1986.

Ollman, Bertell. *Alienation: Marx's Conception of Man in Capitalist Society.* 2d ed. Cambridge: Cambridge University Press, 1976.

O'Neill, John. *For Marx Against Althusser.* Washington, D.C.: University Press of America, 1982.

Padover, Saul K. *Karl Marx: An Intimate Biography.* New York: McGraw-Hill, 1978.

Pedersen, Johannes. *Israel: Its Life and Culture.* 4 vols. Trans. Mrs. Aslaug Moller. London: Oxford University Press, 1926–47.

Phelan, Shane. *Identity Politics: Lesbian Feminism and the Limits of Community.* Philadelphia: Temple University Press, 1989.

Reagon, Bernice Johnson. "Coalition Politics: Turning the Century." In *Home Girls: A Black Feminist Anthology,* ed. Barbara Smith. New York: Kitchen Table Press, 1983.

Reznikoff, Charles. *Poems 1918–1936.* Ed. Seamus Cooney. Santa Barbara, Calif.: Black Sparrow Press, 1976.

Ricoeur, Paul. *Hermeneutics and the Human Sciences: Essays on Language, Action, and Interpretation.* Ed. John B. Thompson. Cambridge: Cambridge University Press, 1981.

Rotenstreich, Nathan. *Jews and German Philosophy.* New York: Schocken Books, 1984.

Sartre, Jean-Paul. *Anti-Semite and Jew.* Trans. George J. Becker. New York: Schocken Books, 1948.

Scholem, Gershon G. *Major Trends in Jewish Mysticism.* New York: Schocken Books, 1954.

Schwartz, Joel. "Liberalism and the Jewish Connection." *Political Theory,* Feb. 1985, 58–84.

Seigel, Jerrold. *Marx's Fate: The Shape of a Life.* Princeton: Princeton University Press, 1978.

Smith, Steven B. *Reading Althusser.* Ithaca, N.Y.: Cornell University Press, 1984.

Spelman, Elizabeth V. *Inessential Woman.* Boston: Beacon Press, 1988.

Tan, Amy. "The Language of Discretion." In *The State of the Language*, ed. Christopher Ricks and Leonard Michaels. Berkeley: University of California Press, 1990.

Taylor, Charles. *Hegel.* Cambridge: Cambridge University Press, 1975.

Taylor, Henry Osborn. *The Classical Heritage of the Middle Ages.* New York: Frederick Ungar Publishing Co., 1957.

Thompson, E. P. *The Poverty of Theory.* London: Merlin Press, 1978.

Walzer, Michael. *Exodus and Revolution.* New York: Basic Books, 1985.

Wartofsky, Marx W. *Feuerbach.* Cambridge: Cambridge University Press, 1977.

Waskow, Arthur I. *Godwrestling.* New York: Schocken Books, 1978.

Wolff, Robert Paul. *Moneybags Must Be So Lucky: On the Literary Structure of Marx's "Capital."* Amherst: University of Massachusetts Press, 1988.

Wright, Addison G. "The Literary Genre Midrash." *Catholic Biblical Quarterly* 28 (1966): 106–38, 417–57.

Wyschogrod, Michael. *The Body of Faith.* New York: Seabury Press, 1983.

Yerushalmi, Yosef Hayim. *Zakhor: Jewish History and Jewish Memory.* Seattle: University of Washington Press, 1982.

Index